The 19th-Century British Novel

Tiny Topic Readers Humanities

Edited by
Bee Lehman and Emily Cole

Volume 1

The 19th-Century British Novel

Edited by
Daniel Dougherty

DE GRUYTER
OLDENBOURG

This series' designers are committed to providing small readers with public domain material for survey courses in the Humanities disciplines, such as English and History. The goal is to have experts provide small selections of materials at low – or no – cost, which instructors can use for their course curriculum.

If you're interested in participating in the project, reach out to the series editors.

This series was designed in connection with Boston College's Collaborative Digital Projects Lab with funding from the Institute for Liberal Arts.

Series Editor: Bee Lehman, Ph.D. and Dr. Emily Cole
Graphic Design: Franzi Paetzold and Dr. Emily Cole.

ISBN 978-3-11-156056-4
e-ISBN (PDF) 978-3-11-156154-7
e-ISBN (EPUB) 978-3-11-156204-9
ISSN 2944-1552

Library of Congress Control Number: 2025901317

Bibliographic information published by the Deutsche Nationalbibliothek
The Deutsche Nationalbibliothek lists this publication in the Deutsche Nationalbibliografie; detailed bibliographic data are available on the internet at http://dnb.dnb.de.

© 2025 Walter de Gruyter GmbH, Berlin/Boston, Genthiner Straße 13, 10785 Berlin
Cover image: Joseph Mallord William Turner (British, London 1775–1851 London), Whalers, ca 1845, oil on canvas, 91.8x122.6cm, The Metropolitan Museum of Art, Catharine Lorillard Wolfe Collection, Wolfe Fund, 1896 (Object number: 96.29), Creative Commons Zero (CC0).
Typesetting: Integra Software Services Pvt. Ltd.

www.degruyter.com
Questions about General Product Safety Regulation:
productsafety@degruyterbrill.com

Image 1: John Leech, Cartoon No, 1: "Substance and Shadow" from *Punch; Or, The London Charivari*, 1841.

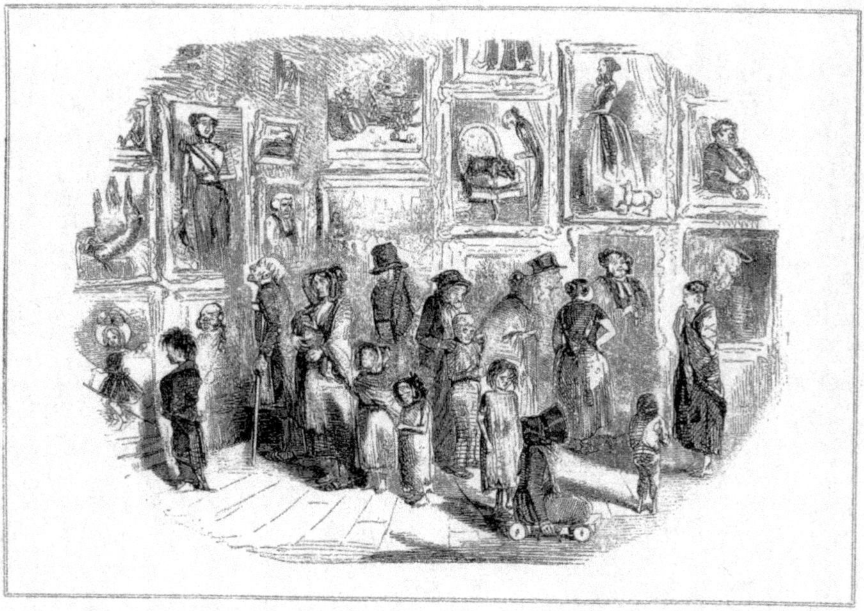

Contents

Images and Illustrations —— IX

Introduction to British Literature in the Nineteenth Century —— 1

Pre-Victorian Novels

Jane Austen's *Pride and Prejudice* —— 6
    Chapter I —— **7**
    Chapter II —— **9**

Mary Shelley's *Frankenstein* —— 11
    Letter 4 —— **12**

Additional Novels —— 18

Early Victorian Novels

Charlotte Brontë's *Jane Eyre* —— 22
    Chapter II —— **23**

William Makepeace Thackeray's *Vanity Fair* —— 29
    Before the Curtain —— **30**
    Chapter I —— **31**
        Chiswick Mall —— **31**

Charles Dickens' *David Copperfield* —— 38
    Chapter I —— **39**
        I Am Born —— **39**

Lewis Carroll's *Alice's Adventures in Wonderland* —— 49
    Chapter VII —— **50**
        A Mad Tea Party —— **50**

Additional Novels —— 56

Late Victorian Novels

George Eliot's *Middlemarch* —— 60
    Prelude —— 61
    Chapter XXIX —— 62

Oscar Wilde's *The Picture of Dorian Gray* —— 69
    The Preface —— 70
    Chapter I —— 71

H.G. Wells' *The Time Machine* —— 81
    Chapter IV —— 82
        Time Travelling —— 82

Joseph Conrad's *Lord Jim* —— 87
    Chapter IV —— 88

Additional Novels —— 92

Secondary Texts —— 93

Further Reading —— 95

Online Resources and Databases —— 97

Appendix I: Timeline of England's Wars —— 99

Appendix II: England's Domestic Timeline —— 101

Editor's Statement —— 103

Index —— 105

Images and Illustrations

Image 1	John Leech, Cartoon No, 1: "Substance and Shadow," 1843, illustration 17.7 x 24.3 cm, In *Punch; Or, The London Charivari* 5 (July 1841): 23, HathiTrust.	Public Domain —— VI
Image 2	Phiz, "The Marshalsea Becomes an Orphan," 1856, illustration, In Charles Dickens, *Little Dorrit* (London: Chapman & Hall, 1856), 351, HathiTrust.	Public Domain —— 1
Image 3	Henry Lark Pratt, "Chatsworth House, Derbyshire," 1852, oil on canvas, 67.5 x 94 cm, 1852, Buxton Museum & Art Gallery.	CC BY, courtesy of Buxton Museum & Art —— 4
Image 4	Hugh Thomson, "She is Tolerable," 1894, illustration, In *Pride and Prejudice*, by Jane Austen (London: George Allen, 1894), HathiTrust.	Public Domain —— 6
Image 5	Frontispiece in Mary Wollstonecraft Shelley, *Frankenstein, or, The Modern Prometheus*, vol. 1, 4 vols., Eng (London: Henry Colburn and Richard Bentley, New Burlington Street, Bell and Bradfute, Edinburgh, and Cumming, Dublin, 1831), HathiTrust.	Public Domain —— 11
Image 6	Joseph Mallord William Turner, "The Fighting Temeraire," 1839, oil on canvas, 90.7 x 121.6 cm, NG524, National Gallery, London.	Public Domain —— 20
Image 7	F.H. Townsend, "'How Dare I, Mrs. Reed? How Dare I? Because It Is the Truth,'" 1898, illustration, In *Jane Eyre: An Autobiography*, by Charlotte Brontë (New York: G.P. Putnam's sons, 1898), HathiTrust.	Public Domain —— 22
Image 8	Frontispiece, In William Makepeace Thackeray, *Vanity Fair: A Novel Without a Hero* (London: Bradbury and Evans, 1849), HathiTrust.	Public Domain —— 29
Image 9	Frontispiece, In Charles Dickens, *David Copperfield*, 2 vols. (Philadelphia: T.B. Peterson, 1850), Internet Archive.	Public Domain —— 38
Image 10	John Tenniel, No. 25, 1864, illustration, In *Alice in Wonderland*, by Lewis Carroll (Mount Vernon, NY: Peter Pauper press, 1940), 94, HathiTrust.	Public Domain —— 49
Image 11	John O'Connor, "The Embankment," 1874, oil on canvas, 92.0 x 142.8 cm, 85.552, London Museum.	Public Domain, courtesy of London Museum —— 58
Image 12	Jessica Landseer, "Village Scene," 1817, oil on canvas, 35.6 x 44.5 cm, B1986.11.2, Yale Center for British Art, Paul Mellon Fund.	Public Domain, courtesy of Yale Center for British Art —— 60
Image 13	Aubrey Beardsley, "The Climax," 1893, illustration, In *The Art of Aubrey Beardsley*, by Arthur Symons (New York: Boni and Liveright, inc., 1918), HathiTrust.	Public Domain —— 69
Image 14	James Abbott McNeill Whistler, "Nocturne in Black and Gold, the Falling Rocket," 1875, oil on panel, 60.3 x 46.7 cm, 46.309, Detroit Institute of Arts Museum.	Public Domain —— 81
Image 15	John Martin, John Martin, "Sadak in Search of the Waters of Oblivion," 1812, oil on canvas, 76.2 x 63.5 cm, Saint Louis Art Museum.	Public Domain —— 87

Introduction to British Literature in the Nineteenth Century

Image 2: Phiz, "The Marshalsea Becomes an Orphan," illustration in Charles Dickens, *Little Dorrit* (London: Chapman & Hall, 1856), 351.

The 19th century in England was a time of incredible experimentation in the form and content of the novel. Detective stories, science fiction, ghost stories, historical novels, and the marriage plot took on manifold guises to fit the rapidly changing world in England and abroad. The population of London grew from 1.4 million in 1815 to 6.5 million in 1900. Literacy amongst men and women reached almost ninety percent by 1870, and the voracious reading public consumed novels through lending libraries, periodicals, and literary magazines such as *Household Words*. The plots of the great British novels are famous and bizarre: wives are locked away in attics, vampires invade London, jewel thefts are committed under the effects of opium, and ghosts visit in the dark of night. All the while, authors wondered what it meant to write to an eager public, and how to adapt their fiction to the onset of modern life not only in London but across the nation: railroads proliferated at a rapid pace, and the rhythms of agricultural time were replaced by the regimen of clock ticks.

Visions of the future or snapshots of the past reveal not only the aspirations of the authors in question but also very real fears of what 'British' and 'Victorian' would come to mean decades after their era ended. Tales of upper-class and aristocratic characters gave way to shocking and earnest depictions of the realities of lower- and middle-class life. Characters succeed and thrive or fail at the capricious whims of their storytellers, often within the stretch of a few dozen pages. Charles Dickens, trafficking in the melodrama he is so famous for, willed absolute good and evil into being with the stroke of his pen, and in the same magazine Elizabeth Gaskell complicated the relationship between workers and owners half a decade later. Protagonists can be superlative, Sherlock Holmes and his like, or superlative for their plainess, Jane Eyre or David Copperfield. Narratives can be impossible and convoluted in one breath, and depict the shocking and all-too-real squalor of the London poor in the next. Social commentary may come from a parliamentary debate, or the birth of a monster. Uniquely of their moment, complicated, and rich, the 19th Century British novels endure into the present with all their eccentricities intact. In all cases the novels included in this reader are, in a word, unforgettable.

Pre-Victorian Novels

Image 3: Henry Lark Pratt, "Chatsworth House, Derbyshire," 1852.

Before Victoria's ascent to the throne in 1837, England saw changes at home and abroad which would shape the coming century. The Acts of Union brought England and Ireland together under one flag in 1801. By 1810, George III had entered his period of insanity and his son George IV had begun acting as ruler, before he officially took the throne in 1820. Militarily, England defeated Spain and France at the Battle of Trafalgar in 1805, and fought in the Napoleonic Wars, among others. The French Revolution weighed heavily on philosophers and authors across the European continent, but for the most part the novels of the first third of the century don't reflect the acute realities of the twin revolutions – industrial and philosophical – which would become all the more apparent as the century progressed. In 1832, the first Reform Act was passed, nearly doubling the size of the electorate, redistricting the nation away from 'rotten boroughs', districts controlled by the crown or wealthy aristocrats who hoarded parliamentary power. In 1833, slavery was abolished throughout the British Empire. In 1837, Victoria, only 18 at the time, became Queen. Jane Austen, a pivotal figure bridging the eighteenth and nineteenth centuries, portrayed miniature societies which grappled with the problems of the middle- and upper-classes of the last century, namely land ownership and suitable marriage matches, while also imbuing her heroines with the fiercely independent spark which would become the hallmark of the nineteenth century literary hero. Mary Shelley's famous *Frankenstein* would pave the way for two centuries of speculative fiction, and Sir Walter Scott would pen *Waverley* in perhaps the finest of the many British historical novels which populated the rest of the century.

Jane Austen's *Pride and Prejudice*

Printed in 1813 in London. Available on Project Gutenberg at https://www.gutenberg.org/ebooks/1342 [last access 27.11.2024].

Image 4: Hugh Thomson, "She is Tolerable," illustration in *Pride and Prejudice*, by Jane Austen (London: George Allen, 1894).

About *Pride and Prejudice*
Jane Austen's 1813 masterpiece *Pride and Prejudice* has delighted readers for centuries and has been adapted as much as any novel of the period across films, television series, and many other mediums. Austen was born in 1775 and died in 1817, and achieved limited success in her lifetime that would only grow as time has passed. She published four novels during her lifetime, *Sense and Sensibility* (1811), *Pride and Prejudice* (1813), *Mansfield Park* (1814), and *Emma* (1816), and two of

https://doi.org/10.1515/9783111561547-003

her unpublished novels *Northanger Abbey* (published 1817, written in 1803) and *Persuasion* (published 1817) were published posthumously. Austen's novels provide commentary on the landed gentry in the late-eighteenth century into the early-nineteenth century, and her plots center on precocious young women finding footing on the marriage market as they navigate its perils and pitfalls in pursuit of economic security and good social standing. Austen's hallmark style, her use of realism, free indirect discourse, and a witty, biting, irony in her prose are all on display in these opening pages of *Pride and Prejudice*.

And on to the novel . . .

Chapter I

It is a truth universally acknowledged, that a single man in possession of a good fortune must be in want of a wife.

However little known the feelings or views of such a man may be on his first entering a neighbourhood, this truth is so well fixed in the minds of the surrounding families, that he is considered as the rightful property of some one or other of their daughters.

"My dear Mr. Bennet," said his lady to him one day, "have you heard that Netherfield Park is let at last?"

Mr. Bennet replied that he had not.

"But it is," returned she; "for Mrs. Long has just been here, and she told me all about it."

Mr. Bennet made no answer.

"Do not you want to know who has taken it?" cried his wife, impatiently.

"*You* want to tell me, and I have no objection to hearing it."

This was invitation enough.

"Why, my dear, you must know, Mrs. Long says that Netherfield is taken by a young man of large fortune from the north of England; that he came down on Monday in a chaise and four to see the place, and was so much delighted with it that he agreed with Mr. Morris immediately; that he is to take possession before Michaelmas, and some of his servants are to be in the house by the end of next week."

"What is his name?"

"Bingley."

"Is he married or single?"

"Oh, single, my dear, to be sure! A single man of large fortune; four or five thousand a year. What a fine thing for our girls!"

"How so? how can it affect them?"

"My dear Mr. Bennet," replied his wife, "how can you be so tiresome? You must know that I am thinking of his marrying one of them."

"Is that his design in settling here?"

"Design? Nonsense, how can you talk so! But it is very likely that he *may* fall in love with one of them, and therefore you must visit him as soon as he comes."

"I see no occasion for that. You and the girls may go – or you may send them by themselves, which perhaps will be still better; for as you are as handsome as any of them, Mr. Bingley might like you the best of the party."

"My dear, you flatter me. I certainly *have* had my share of beauty, but I do not pretend to be anything extraordinary now. When a woman has five grown-up daughters, she ought to give over thinking of her own beauty."

"In such cases, a woman has not often much beauty to think of."

"But, my dear, you must indeed go and see Mr. Bingley when he comes into the neighbourhood."

"It is more than I engage for, I assure you."

"But consider your daughters. Only think what an establishment it would be for one of them. Sir William and Lady Lucas are determined to go, merely on that account; for in general, you know, they visit no new comers. Indeed you must go, for it will be impossible for *us* to visit him, if you do not."

"You are over scrupulous, surely. I dare say Mr. Bingley will be very glad to see you; and I will send a few lines by you to assure him of my hearty consent to his marrying whichever he chooses of the girls – though I must throw in a good word for my little Lizzy."

"I desire you will do no such thing. Lizzy is not a bit better than the others: and I am sure she is not half so handsome as Jane, nor half so good-humoured as Lydia. But you are always giving *her* the preference."

"They have none of them much to recommend them," replied he: "they are all silly and ignorant like other girls; but Lizzy has something more of quickness than her sisters."

"Mr. Bennet, how can you abuse your own children in such a way? You take delight in vexing me. You have no compassion on my poor nerves."

"You mistake me, my dear. I have a high respect for your nerves. They are my old friends. I have heard you mention them with consideration these twenty years at least."

"Ah, you do not know what I suffer."

"But I hope you will get over it, and live to see many young men of four thousand a year come into the neighbourhood."

"It will be no use to us, if twenty such should come, since you will not visit them."

"Depend upon it, my dear, that when there are twenty, I will visit them all."

Mr. Bennet was so odd a mixture of quick parts, sarcastic humour, reserve, and caprice, that the experience of three-and-twenty years had been insufficient to make his wife understand his character. *Her* mind was less difficult to develope. She was a woman of mean understanding, little information, and uncertain temper. When she was discontented, she fancied herself nervous. The business of her life was to get her daughters married: its solace was visiting and news.

Chapter II

Mr. Bennet was among the earliest of those who waited on Mr. Bingley. He had always intended to visit him, though to the last always assuring his wife that he should not go; and till the evening after the visit was paid she had no knowledge of it. It was then disclosed in the following manner. Observing his second daughter employed in trimming a hat, he suddenly addressed her with, –

"I hope Mr. Bingley will like it, Lizzy."

"We are not in a way to know *what* Mr. Bingley likes," said her mother, resentfully, "since we are not to visit."

"But you forget, mamma," said Elizabeth, "that we shall meet him at the assemblies, and that Mrs. Long has promised to introduce him."

"I do not believe Mrs. Long will do any such thing. She has two nieces of her own. She is a selfish, hypocritical woman, and I have no opinion of her."

"No more have I," said Mr. Bennet; "and I am glad to find that you do not depend on her serving you."

Mrs. Bennet deigned not to make any reply; but, unable to contain herself, began scolding one of her daughters.

"Don't keep coughing so, Kitty, for heaven's sake! Have a little compassion on my nerves. You tear them to pieces."

"Kitty has no discretion in her coughs," said her father; "she times them ill."

"I do not cough for my own amusement," replied Kitty, fretfully. "When is your next ball to be, Lizzy?"

"To-morrow fortnight."

"Ay, so it is," cried her mother, "and Mrs. Long does not come back till the day before; so, it will be impossible for her to introduce him, for she will not know him herself."

"Then, my dear, you may have the advantage of your friend, and introduce Mr. Bingley to *her*."

"Impossible, Mr. Bennet, impossible, when I am not acquainted with him myself; how can you be so teasing?"

"I honour your circumspection. A fortnight's acquaintance is certainly very little. One cannot know what a man really is by the end of a fortnight. But if *we* do not venture, somebody else will; and after all, Mrs. Long and her nieces must stand their chance; and, therefore, as she will think it an act of kindness, if you decline the office, I will take it on myself."

The girls stared at their father. Mrs. Bennet said only, "Nonsense, nonsense!"

"What can be the meaning of that emphatic exclamation?" cried he. "Do you consider the forms of introduction, and the stress that is laid on them, as nonsense? I cannot quite agree with you *there*. What say you, Mary? For you are a young lady of deep reflection, I know, and read great books, and make extracts."

Mary wished to say something very sensible, but knew not how.

"While Mary is adjusting her ideas," he continued, "let us return to Mr. Bingley."

"I am sick of Mr. Bingley," cried his wife.

"I am sorry to hear *that*; but why did you not tell me so before? If I had known as much this morning, I certainly would not have called on him. It is very unlucky; but as I have actually paid the visit, we cannot escape the acquaintance now."

The astonishment of the ladies was just what he wished – that of Mrs. Bennet perhaps surpassing the rest; though when the first tumult of joy was over, she began to declare that it was what she had expected all the while.

"How good it was in you, my dear Mr. Bennet! But I knew I should persuade you at last. I was sure you loved your girls too well to neglect such an acquaintance. Well, how pleased I am! And it is such a good joke, too, that you should have gone this morning, and never said a word about it till now."

"Now, Kitty, you may cough as much as you choose," said Mr. Bennet; and, as he spoke, he left the room, fatigued with the raptures of his wife.

"What an excellent father you have, girls," said she, when the door was shut. "I do not know how you will ever make him amends for his kindness; or me either, for that matter. At our time of life, it is not so pleasant, I can tell you, to be making new acquaintances every day; but for your sakes we would do anything. Lydia, my love, though you *are* the youngest, I dare say Mr. Bingley will dance with you at the next ball."

"Oh," said Lydia, stoutly, "I am not afraid; for though I *am* the youngest, I'm the tallest."

The rest of the evening was spent in conjecturing how soon he would return Mr. Bennet's visit, and determining when they should ask him to dinner.

Mary Shelley's *Frankenstein*

First published in 1818 in London. Available full text on Project Gutenberg, https://www.gutenberg.org/ebooks/84 [last access 27.11.2024].

Image 5: Frontispiece in Mary Wollstonecraft Shelley, *Frankenstein, or, The Modern Prometheus*, vol. 1, 4 vols. (London: Henry Colburn and Richard Bentley, New Burlington Street, Bell and Bradfute, Edinburgh, and Cumming, Dublin, 1831).

> **About *Frankenstein***
> Mary Shelley was born in 1797 and died in 1851, the daughter of philosopher William Godwin and women's rights activist Mary Wollstonecraft. She began a romance with the already-married poet Percy Bysshe Shelley in 1814, and would go on to marry him several years later after his first wife's suicide. In 1816, Mary Shelley, her husband Percy, John Polidori, and Lord Byron challenged each other, on vacation near Lake Geneva, to write a ghost story. A volcanic eruption at Mount Tambora had caused unusual weather: the year seemingly lacked a summer season, and the writers found themselves shut indoors despite the time of year. So the story goes, unable to think of a suitable ghost tale, Mary Shelley dreamed of a monstrous scientist and a creature he brings to life. The rest, of course, is history. *Frankenstein* is considered by some to be the earliest work of science fiction, and is a classic of Gothic literature and horror fiction. Its structure is worth commenting on: *Frankenstein* is an epistolary novel, told through (fictional) documents passed between Captain Robert Walton and his sister Margaret Walton, and its embedded frame narrative increases the layers of intrigue and mystique at the center of its famous contemplation of what it might mean to be human, and what it means to be truly monstrous.
>
> *And on to the novel . . .*

Letter 4

To Mrs. Saville, England. August 5th, 17 – .
So strange an accident has happened to us that I cannot forbear recording it, although it is very probable that you will see me before these papers can come into your possession.

Last Monday (July 31st) we were nearly surrounded by ice, which closed in the ship on all sides, scarcely leaving her the sea-room in which she floated. Our situation was somewhat dangerous, especially as we were compassed round by a very thick fog. We accordingly lay to, hoping that some change would take place in the atmosphere and weather.

About two o'clock the mist cleared away, and we beheld, stretched out in every direction, vast and irregular plains of ice, which seemed to have no end. Some of my comrades groaned, and my own mind began to grow watchful with anxious thoughts, when a strange sight suddenly attracted our attention and diverted our solicitude from our own situation. We perceived a low carriage, fixed on a sledge and drawn by dogs, pass on towards the north, at the distance of half a mile; a being which had the shape of a man, but apparently of gigantic stature, sat in the sledge and guided the dogs. We watched the rapid progress of the traveller with our telescopes until he was lost among the distant inequalities of the ice.

This appearance excited our unqualified wonder. We were, as we believed, many hundred miles from any land; but this apparition seemed to denote that it was not, in reality, so distant as we had supposed. Shut in, however, by ice, it was impossible to follow his track, which we had observed with the greatest attention.

About two hours after this occurrence we heard the ground sea, and before night the ice broke and freed our ship. We, however, lay to until the morning, fearing to encounter in the dark those large loose masses which float about after the breaking up of the ice. I profited of this time to rest for a few hours.

In the morning, however, as soon as it was light, I went upon deck and found all the sailors busy on one side of the vessel, apparently talking to someone in the sea. It was, in fact, a sledge, like that we had seen before, which had drifted towards us in the night on a large fragment of ice. Only one dog remained alive; but there was a human being within it whom the sailors were persuading to enter the vessel. He was not, as the other traveller seemed to be, a savage inhabitant of some undiscovered island, but a European. When I appeared on deck the master said, "Here is our captain, and he will not allow you to perish on the open sea."

On perceiving me, the stranger addressed me in English, although with a foreign accent. "Before I come on board your vessel," said he, "will you have the kindness to inform me whither you are bound?"

You may conceive my astonishment on hearing such a question addressed to me from a man on the brink of destruction and to whom I should have supposed that my vessel would have been a resource which he would not have exchanged for the most precious wealth the earth can afford. I replied, however, that we were on a voyage of discovery towards the northern pole.

Upon hearing this he appeared satisfied and consented to come on board. Good God! Margaret, if you had seen the man who thus capitulated for his safety, your surprise would have been boundless. His limbs were nearly frozen, and his body dreadfully emaciated by fatigue and suffering. I never saw a man in so wretched a condition. We attempted to carry him into the cabin, but as soon as he had quitted the fresh air he fainted. We accordingly brought him back to the deck and restored him to animation by rubbing him with brandy and forcing him to swallow a small quantity. As soon as he showed signs of life we wrapped him up in blankets and placed him near the chimney of the kitchen stove. By slow degrees he recovered and ate a little soup, which restored him wonderfully.

Two days passed in this manner before he was able to speak, and I often feared that his sufferings had deprived him of understanding. When he had in some measure recovered, I removed him to my own cabin and attended on him as much as my duty would permit. I never saw a more interesting creature: his eyes have generally an expression of wildness, and even madness, but there are moments when, if anyone performs an act of kindness towards him or does him any the most trifling service, his whole countenance is lighted up, as it were, with a beam of benevolence and sweetness that I never saw equalled. But he is generally melancholy and despairing, and sometimes he gnashes his teeth, as if impatient of the weight of woes that oppresses him.

When my guest was a little recovered I had great trouble to keep off the men, who wished to ask him a thousand questions; but I would not allow him to be tormented by their idle curiosity, in a state of body and mind whose restoration evidently depended upon entire repose. Once, however, the lieutenant asked why he had come so far upon the ice in so strange a vehicle.

His countenance instantly assumed an aspect of the deepest gloom, and he replied, "To seek one who fled from me."

"And did the man whom you pursued travel in the same fashion?"

"Yes."

"Then I fancy we have seen him, for the day before we picked you up we saw some dogs drawing a sledge, with a man in it, across the ice."

This aroused the stranger's attention, and he asked a multitude of questions concerning the route which the dæmon, as he called him, had pursued. Soon after, when he was alone with me, he said, "I have, doubtless, excited your curiosity, as well as that of these good people; but you are too considerate to make inquiries."

"Certainly; it would indeed be very impertinent and inhuman in me to trouble you with any inquisitiveness of mine."

"And yet you rescued me from a strange and perilous situation; you have benevolently restored me to life."

Soon after this he inquired if I thought that the breaking up of the ice had destroyed the other sledge. I replied that I could not answer with any degree of certainty, for the ice had not broken until near midnight, and the traveller might have arrived at a place of safety before that time; but of this I could not judge.

From this time a new spirit of life animated the decaying frame of the stranger. He manifested the greatest eagerness to be upon deck to watch for the sledge which had before appeared; but I have persuaded him to remain in the cabin, for he is far too weak to sustain the rawness of the atmosphere. I have promised that someone should watch for him and give him instant notice if any new object should appear in sight.

Such is my journal of what relates to this strange occurrence up to the present day. The stranger has gradually improved in health but is very silent and appears uneasy when anyone except myself enters his cabin. Yet his manners are so conciliating and gentle that the sailors are all interested in him, although they have had very little communication with him. For my own part, I begin to love him as a brother, and his constant and deep grief fills me with sympathy and compassion. He must have been a noble creature in his better days, being even now in wreck so attractive and amiable.

I said in one of my letters, my dear Margaret, that I should find no friend on the wide ocean; yet I have found a man who, before his spirit had been broken by misery, I should have been happy to have possessed as the brother of my heart.

I shall continue my journal concerning the stranger at intervals, should I have any fresh incidents to record.

August 13th, 17 – .

My affection for my guest increases every day. He excites at once my admiration and my pity to an astonishing degree. How can I see so noble a creature destroyed by misery without feeling the most poignant grief? He is so gentle, yet so wise; his mind is so cultivated, and when he speaks, although his words are culled with the choicest art, yet they flow with rapidity and unparalleled eloquence.

He is now much recovered from his illness and is continually on the deck, apparently watching for the sledge that preceded his own. Yet, although unhappy, he is not so utterly occupied by his own misery but that he interests himself deeply in the projects of others. He has frequently conversed with me on mine, which I have communicated to him without disguise. He entered attentively into all my arguments in favour of my eventual success and into every minute detail of the measures I had taken to secure it. I was easily led by the sympathy which he evinced to use the language of my heart, to give utterance to the burning ardour of my soul and to say, with all the fervour that warmed me, how gladly I would sacrifice my fortune, my existence, my every hope, to the furtherance of my enterprise. One man's life or death were but a small price to pay for the acquirement of the knowledge which I sought, for the dominion I should acquire and transmit over the elemental foes of our race. As I spoke, a dark gloom spread over my listener's countenance. At first I perceived that he tried to suppress his emotion; he placed his hands before his eyes, and my voice quivered and failed me as I beheld tears trickle fast from between his fingers; a groan burst from his heaving breast. I paused; at length he spoke, in broken accents: "Unhappy man! Do you share my madness? Have you drunk also of the intoxicating draught? Hear me; let me reveal my tale, and you will dash the cup from your lips!"

Such words, you may imagine, strongly excited my curiosity; but the paroxysm of grief that had seized the stranger overcame his weakened powers, and many hours of repose and tranquil conversation were necessary to restore his composure.

Having conquered the violence of his feelings, he appeared to despise himself for being the slave of passion; and quelling the dark tyranny of despair, he led me again to converse concerning myself personally. He asked me the history of my earlier years. The tale was quickly told, but it awakened various trains of reflection. I spoke of my desire of finding a friend, of my thirst for a more intimate sympathy with a fellow mind than had ever fallen to my lot, and expressed my conviction that a man could boast of little happiness who did not enjoy this blessing.

"I agree with you," replied the stranger; "we are unfashioned creatures, but half made up, if one wiser, better, dearer than ourselves – such a friend ought to be – do not lend his aid to perfectionate our weak and faulty natures. I once had a friend, the most noble of human creatures, and am entitled, therefore, to judge respecting friendship. You have hope, and the world before you, and have no cause for despair. But I – I have lost everything and cannot begin life anew."

As he said this his countenance became expressive of a calm, settled grief that touched me to the heart. But he was silent and presently retired to his cabin.

Even broken in spirit as he is, no one can feel more deeply than he does the beauties of nature. The starry sky, the sea, and every sight afforded by these wonderful regions seem still to have the power of elevating his soul from earth. Such a man has a double existence: he may suffer misery and be overwhelmed by disappointments, yet when he has retired into himself, he will be like a celestial spirit that has a halo around him, within whose circle no grief or folly ventures.

Will you smile at the enthusiasm I express concerning this divine wanderer? You would not if you saw him. You have been tutored and refined by books and retirement from the world, and you are therefore somewhat fastidious; but this only renders you the more fit to appreciate the extraordinary merits of this wonderful man. Sometimes I have endeavoured to discover what quality it is which he possesses that elevates him so immeasurably above any other person I ever knew. I believe it to be an intuitive discernment, a quick but never-failing power of judgment, a penetration into the causes of things, unequalled for clearness and precision; add to this a facility of expression and a voice whose varied intonations are soul-subduing music.

August 19th, 17 – .

Yesterday the stranger said to me, "You may easily perceive, Captain Walton, that I have suffered great and unparalleled misfortunes. I had determined at one time that the memory of these evils should die with me, but you have won me to alter my determination. You seek for knowledge and wisdom, as I once did; and I ardently hope that the gratification of your wishes may not be a serpent to sting you, as mine has been. I do not know that the relation of my disasters will be useful to you; yet, when I reflect that you are pursuing the same course, exposing yourself to the same dangers which have rendered me what I am, I imagine that you may deduce an apt moral from my tale, one that may direct you if you succeed in your undertaking and console you in case of failure. Prepare to hear of occurrences which are usually deemed marvellous. Were we among the tamer scenes of nature I might fear to encounter your unbelief, perhaps your ridicule; but many things will appear possible in these wild and mysterious regions which would provoke the laughter of those unacquainted with the ever-varied powers of nature; nor can I doubt but that my tale conveys in its series internal evidence of the truth of the events of which it is composed."

You may easily imagine that I was much gratified by the offered communication, yet I could not endure that he should renew his grief by a recital of his misfortunes. I felt the greatest eagerness to hear the promised narrative, partly from curiosity and partly from a strong desire to ameliorate his fate if it were in my power. I expressed these feelings in my answer.

"I thank you," he replied, "for your sympathy, but it is useless; my fate is nearly fulfilled. I wait but for one event, and then I shall repose in peace. I understand your feeling," continued he, perceiving that I wished to interrupt him; "but you are mistaken, my friend, if thus you will allow me to name you; nothing can alter my destiny; listen to my history, and you will perceive how irrevocably it is determined."

He then told me that he would commence his narrative the next day when I should be at leisure. This promise drew from me the warmest thanks. I have resolved every night, when I am not imperatively occupied by my duties, to record, as nearly as possible in his own words, what he has related during the day. If I should be engaged, I will at least make notes. This manuscript will doubtless afford you the greatest pleasure; but to me, who know him, and who hear it from his own lips – with what interest and sympathy shall I read it in some future day! Even now, as I commence my task, his full-toned voice swells in my ears; his lustrous eyes dwell on me with all their melancholy sweetness; I see his thin hand raised in animation, while the lineaments of his face are irradiated by the soul within. Strange and harrowing must be his story, frightful the storm which embraced the gallant vessel on its course and wrecked it – thus!

Additional Novels

Edgeworth, Maria. *Castle Rackrent*. London, 1800. Project Gutenberg, https://www.gutenberg.org/ebooks/1424/ [last access 27.11.2024].

Scott, Walter. *Waverley*. London, 1814. Project Gutenberg. https://www.gutenberg.org/ebooks/5998/ [last access 27.11.2024].

Austen, Jane. *Emma*. London, 1815. Project Gutenberg. https://www.gutenberg.org/ebooks/158/ [last access 27.11.2024].

Early Victorian Novels

Image 6: J.M.W. Turner, "The Fighting Téméraire," 1839.

Queen Victoria's ascent to the throne in 1837 was a watershed moment not only for the English, but also for people around the world. During her reign – which spanned nearly sixty-five years – England was perpetually engaged in at least one war, and typically several, whether on land or at sea. The British Empire flourished, growing seemingly without end, and the Victorian period felt like an epoch that might last forever. Technology boomed: railroads crisscrossed England, the telephone was invented, and the entire nation was synched to national time kept by clocktowers all set to the same standard, all before Victoria entered middle age. Literacy expanded across the nation, and a voracious population of readers from all classes emerged looking to consume stories of all kinds. The novel – the genre par excellence of the century – was typically released serially, one part at a time, for about a shilling a month. Likewise, novels circulated through lending libraries, allowing more English citizens than ever to keep up with the latest and most compelling stories. At pubs and on factory floors, novels were read aloud for the entertainment and enjoyment of any who would listen. Still, inequalities compounded year over year, and the deplorable conditions of the London poor became something which politicians and novelists grappled with throughout Victoria's reign.

Authors relied on the biographical form – the chronicling of one individual life – to show the social stratification of London and the nation: the heroine becomes ordinary, but the richness of her mind dazzles readers. Gone are Odysseus and Othello: Brontë's Jane Eyre and Dickens's Pip become the flag bearers of nineteenth century narrative. Children's literature blossomed, and fairy tales were translated and adapted for new generations of children in England. In the novels of the mid-century, the world is full of latent potentiality, the sense that anything is possible and that turns of fortune come in the form of surprise visitors and hidden secrets. Authors begin to reflect on their status as authors both inside and outside of their texts: William Makepeace Thackeray governs *Vanity Fair* with the metaphor of the puppet master performing for a crowd, for example, while Wilkie Collins and Dickens write essays contemplating what they write, why, and, most important of all, for whom?

Charlotte Brontë's *Jane Eyre*

Published in 1847 in London. Available on Project Gutenberg at https://www.gutenberg.org/ebooks/1260/ [last access 27.11.2024].

Image 7: F.H. Townsend, "How dare I, Mrs. Reed? How dare I? Because it is the truth," illustration in *Jane Eyre: An Autobiography*, by Charlotte Brontë (New York: G.P. Putnam's sons, 1898).

https://doi.org/10.1515/9783111561547-007

Jane Eyre
Published under the pen name Currer Bell, Charlotte Brontë's 1847 *Jane Eyre* is styled as the autobiography of Jane Eyre, edited, rather than written, by Bell. Born in 1816 to the Reverend Patrick Brontë, Charlotte would become the de facto mother to her younger siblings after her mother's 1821 death. Always a lover of literature – from fairy tales to *Aesop's Fables* to *The Arabian Nights* – Brontë began her journey as a writer early, writing the *Juvenilia* with her siblings well before publishing any of her work professionally. *Jane Eyre* is her best known novel, and it is exceptional: the dazzling interiority that Jane demonstrates and her powerful voice and sense of conviction give the novel its depth and passion. A *Bildungsroman*, or a coming-of-age novel, the story sees Jane grow from a little orphaned girl to a competent, capable woman who has stood by what she believes in and is, finally, rewarded for doing so. Trafficking in conventions of the Gothic, the fairy tale, and romance, *Jane Eyre* is a book with many twists and turns, and the famous and shocking wedding scene and its aftermath surprise readers today as much as it did in Brontë's time. Brontë would publish other novels before her 1855 death including *Villette* and *Shirley*, but it is *Jane Eyre* that typifies her style and themes best.

Now on to the novel . . .

Chapter II

I resisted all the way: a new thing for me, and a circumstance which greatly strengthened the bad opinion Bessie and Miss Abbot were disposed to entertain of me. The fact is, I was a trifle beside myself; or rather out of myself, as the French would say: I was conscious that a moment's mutiny had already rendered me liable to strange penalties, and, like any other rebel slave, I felt resolved, in my desperation, to go all lengths.

"Hold her arms, Miss Abbot: she's like a mad cat."

"For shame! for shame!" cried the lady's-maid. "What shocking conduct, Miss Eyre, to strike a young gentleman, your benefactress's son! Your young master."

"Master! How is he my master? Am I a servant?"

"No; you are less than a servant, for you do nothing for your keep. There, sit down, and think over your wickedness."

They had got me by this time into the apartment indicated by Mrs. Reed, and had thrust me upon a stool: my impulse was to rise from it like a spring; their two pair of hands arrested me instantly.

"If you don't sit still, you must be tied down," said Bessie. "Miss Abbot, lend me your garters; she would break mine directly."

Miss Abbot turned to divest a stout leg of the necessary ligature. This preparation for bonds, and the additional ignominy it inferred, took a little of the excitement out of me.

"Don't take them off," I cried; "I will not stir."

In guarantee whereof, I attached myself to my seat by my hands.

"Mind you don't," said Bessie; and when she had ascertained that I was really subsiding, she loosened her hold of me; then she and Miss Abbot stood with folded arms, looking darkly and doubtfully on my face, as incredulous of my sanity.

"She never did so before," at last said Bessie, turning to the Abigail.

"But it was always in her," was the reply. "I've told Missis often my opinion about the child, and Missis agreed with me. She's an underhand little thing: I never saw a girl of her age with so much cover."

Bessie answered not; but ere long, addressing me, she said – "You ought to be aware, Miss, that you are under obligations to Mrs. Reed: she keeps you: if she were to turn you off, you would have to go to the poorhouse."

I had nothing to say to these words: they were not new to me: my very first recollections of existence included hints of the same kind. This reproach of my dependence had become a vague sing-song in my ear: very painful and crushing, but only half intelligible. Miss Abbot joined in –

"And you ought not to think yourself on an equality with the Misses Reed and Master Reed, because Missis kindly allows you to be brought up with them. They will have a great deal of money, and you will have none: it is your place to be humble, and to try to make yourself agreeable to them."

"What we tell you is for your good," added Bessie, in no harsh voice, "you should try to be useful and pleasant, then, perhaps, you would have a home here; but if you become passionate and rude, Missis will send you away, I am sure."

"Besides," said Miss Abbot, "God will punish her: He might strike her dead in the midst of her tantrums, and then where would she go? Come, Bessie, we will leave her: I wouldn't have her heart for anything. Say your prayers, Miss Eyre, when you are by yourself; for if you don't repent, something bad might be permitted to come down the chimney and fetch you away."

They went, shutting the door, and locking it behind them.

The red-room was a square chamber, very seldom slept in, I might say never, indeed, unless when a chance influx of visitors at Gateshead Hall rendered it necessary to turn to account all the accommodation it contained: yet it was one of the largest and stateliest chambers in the mansion. A bed supported on massive pillars of mahogany, hung with curtains of deep red damask, stood out like a tabernacle in the centre; the two large windows, with their blinds always drawn down, were half shrouded in festoons and falls of similar drapery; the carpet was red; the table at the foot of the bed was covered with a crimson cloth; the walls were a soft fawn colour with a blush of pink in it; the wardrobe, the toilet-table, the chairs were of darkly polished old mahogany. Out of these deep surrounding shades rose high, and glared white, the piled-up mattresses and pillows of the bed, spread with a snowy Marseilles counterpane. Scarcely less prominent was an ample cushioned easy-chair near the head of the bed, also white, with a footstool before it; and looking, as I thought, like a pale throne.

This room was chill, because it seldom had a fire; it was silent, because remote from the nursery and kitchen; solemn, because it was known to be so seldom entered. The house-maid alone came here on Saturdays, to wipe from the mirrors and the furniture a week's quiet dust: and Mrs. Reed herself, at far intervals, visited it to review the contents of a certain secret drawer in the wardrobe, where were stored divers parchments, her jewel-casket, and a miniature of her deceased husband; and in those last words lies the secret of the red-room – the spell which kept it so lonely in spite of its grandeur.

Mr. Reed had been dead nine years: it was in this chamber he breathed his last; here he lay in state; hence his coffin was borne by the undertaker's men; and, since that day, a sense of dreary consecration had guarded it from frequent intrusion.

My seat, to which Bessie and the bitter Miss Abbot had left me riveted, was a low ottoman near the marble chimney-piece; the bed rose before me; to my right hand there was the high, dark wardrobe, with subdued, broken reflections varying the gloss of its panels; to my left were the muffled windows; a great looking-glass between them repeated the vacant majesty of the bed and room. I was not quite sure whether they had locked the door; and when I dared move, I got up and went to see. Alas! yes: no jail was ever more secure. Returning, I had to cross before the looking-glass; my fascinated glance involuntarily explored the depth it revealed. All looked colder and darker in that visionary hollow than in reality: and the strange little figure there gazing at me, with a white face and arms specking the gloom, and glittering eyes of fear moving where all else was still, had the effect of a real spirit: I thought it like one of the tiny phantoms, half fairy, half imp, Bessie's evening stories represented as coming out of lone, ferny dells in moors, and appearing before the eyes of belated travellers. I returned to my stool.

Superstition was with me at that moment; but it was not yet her hour for complete victory: my blood was still warm; the mood of the revolted slave was still bracing me with its bitter vigour; I had to stem a rapid rush of retrospective thought before I quailed to the dismal present.

All John Reed's violent tyrannies, all his sisters' proud indifference, all his mother's aversion, all the servants' partiality, turned up in my disturbed mind like a dark deposit in a turbid well. Why was I always suffering, always browbeaten, always accused, for ever condemned? Why could I never please? Why was it useless to try to win any one's favour? Eliza, who was headstrong and selfish, was respected. Georgiana, who had a spoiled temper, a very acrid spite, a captious and insolent carriage, was universally indulged. Her beauty, her pink cheeks and golden curls, seemed to give delight to all who looked at her, and to purchase indemnity for every fault. John no one thwarted, much less punished; though he twisted the necks of the pigeons, killed the little pea-chicks, set the dogs at the sheep, stripped the hothouse vines of their fruit, and broke the buds off the choicest plants in the conservatory: he called his mother "old girl," too; sometimes reviled her for her dark skin, similar to his own; bluntly disregarded her wishes; not unfrequently tore and spoiled her silk attire; and he was still "her own darling." I dared commit no fault: I strove to fulfil every duty; and I was termed naughty and tiresome, sullen and sneaking, from morning to noon, and from noon to night.

My head still ached and bled with the blow and fall I had received: no one had reproved John for wantonly striking me; and because I had turned against him to avert farther irrational violence, I was loaded with general opprobrium.

"Unjust! – unjust!" said my reason, forced by the agonising stimulus into precocious though transitory power: and Resolve, equally wrought up, instigated some strange expedient to achieve escape from insupportable oppression – as running away, or, if that could not be effected, never eating or drinking more, and letting myself die.

What a consternation of soul was mine that dreary afternoon! How all my brain was in tumult, and all my heart in insurrection! Yet in what darkness, what dense ignorance, was the mental battle fought! I could not answer the ceaseless inward question – WHY I thus suffered; now, at the distance of – I will not say how many years, I see it clearly.

I was a discord in Gateshead Hall: I was like nobody there; I had nothing in harmony with Mrs. Reed or her children, or her chosen vassalage. If they did not love me, in fact, as little did I love them. They were not bound to regard with affection a thing that could not sympathise with one amongst them; a heterogeneous thing, opposed to them in temperament, in capacity, in propensities; a useless thing, incapable of serving their interest, or adding to their pleasure; a noxious thing, cherishing the germs of indignation at their treatment, of contempt of their judgment. I know that had I been a sanguine, brilliant, careless, exacting, handsome, romping child – though equally dependent and friendless – Mrs. Reed would have endured my presence more complacently; her children would have entertained for me more of the cordiality of fellow-feeling; the servants would have been less prone to make me the scapegoat of the nursery.

Daylight began to forsake the red-room; it was past four o'clock, and the beclouded afternoon was tending to drear twilight. I heard the rain still beating continuously on the staircase window, and the wind howling in the grove behind the hall; I grew by degrees cold as a stone, and then my courage sank. My habitual mood of humiliation, self-doubt, forlorn depression, fell damp on the embers of my decaying ire. All said I was wicked, and perhaps I might be so; what thought had I been but just conceiving of starving myself to death? That certainly was a crime: and was I fit to die? Or was the vault under the chancel of Gateshead Church an inviting bourne? In such vault I had been told did Mr. Reed lie buried; and led by this thought to recall his idea, I dwelt on it with gathering dread. I could not remember him; but I knew that he was my own uncle – my mother's brother – that he had taken me when a parentless infant to his house; and that in his last moments he had required a promise of Mrs. Reed that she would rear and maintain me as one of her own children. Mrs. Reed probably considered she had kept this promise; and so she had, I dare say, as well as her nature would permit her; but how could she really like an interloper not of her race, and unconnected with her, after her husband's death, by any tie? It must have been most irksome to find herself bound by a hard-wrung pledge to stand in the stead of a parent to a strange child she could not love, and to see an uncongenial alien permanently intruded on her own family group.

A singular notion dawned upon me. I doubted not – never doubted – that if Mr. Reed had been alive he would have treated me kindly; and now, as I sat looking at the white bed and overshadowed walls – occasionally also turning a fascinated eye towards the dimly gleaning mirror – I began to recall what I had heard of dead men, troubled in their graves by the violation of their last wishes, revisiting the earth to punish the perjured and avenge the oppressed; and I thought Mr. Reed's spirit, harassed by the wrongs of his sister's child, might quit its abode – whether in the church vault or in the unknown world of the departed – and rise before me in this chamber. I wiped my tears and hushed my sobs, fearful lest any sign of violent grief might waken a preternatural voice to comfort me, or elicit from the gloom some haloed face, bending over me with strange pity. This idea, consolatory in theory, I felt would be terrible if realised: with all my might I endeavoured to stifle it – I endeavoured to be firm. Shaking my hair from my eyes, I lifted my head and tried to look boldly round the dark room; at this moment a light gleamed on the wall. Was it, I asked myself, a ray from the moon penetrating some aperture in the blind? No; moonlight was still, and this stirred; while I gazed, it glided up to the ceiling and quivered over my head. I can now conjecture readily that this streak of light was, in all likelihood, a gleam from a lantern carried by some one across the lawn: but then, prepared as my mind was for horror, shaken as my nerves were by agitation, I thought the swift darting beam was a herald of some coming vision from another world. My heart beat thick, my head grew hot; a sound filled my ears, which I deemed the rushing of wings; something seemed near me; I was oppressed, suffocated: endurance broke down; I rushed to the door and shook the lock in desperate effort. Steps came running along the outer passage; the key turned, Bessie and Abbot entered.

"Miss Eyre, are you ill?" said Bessie.

"What a dreadful noise! it went quite through me!" exclaimed Abbot.

"Take me out! Let me go into the nursery!" was my cry.

"What for? Are you hurt? Have you seen something?" again demanded Bessie.

"Oh! I saw a light, and I thought a ghost would come." I had now got hold of Bessie's hand, and she did not snatch it from me.

"She has screamed out on purpose," declared Abbot, in some disgust. "And what a scream! If she had been in great pain one would have excused it, but she only wanted to bring us all here: I know her naughty tricks."

"What is all this?" demanded another voice peremptorily; and Mrs. Reed came along the corridor, her cap flying wide, her gown rustling stormily. "Abbot and Bessie, I believe I gave orders that Jane Eyre should be left in the red-room till I came to her myself."

"Miss Jane screamed so loud, ma'am," pleaded Bessie.

"Let her go," was the only answer. "Loose Bessie's hand, child: you cannot succeed in getting out by these means, be assured. I abhor artifice, particularly in children; it is my duty to show you that tricks will not answer: you will now stay here an hour longer, and it is only on condition of perfect submission and stillness that I shall liberate you then."

"O aunt! have pity! Forgive me! I cannot endure it – let me be punished some other way! I shall be killed if – "

"Silence! This violence is all most repulsive:" and so, no doubt, she felt it. I was a precocious actress in her eyes; she sincerely looked on me as a compound of virulent passions, mean spirit, and dangerous duplicity.

William Makepeace Thackeray's *Vanity Fair*

Published in 1848 in London. Available on Project Gutenberg at https://www.gutenberg.org/ebooks/599/ [last access 27.11.2024].

Image 8: Frontispiece in William Makepeace Thackeray, *Vanity Fair: A Novel Without a Hero* (London: Bradbury and Evans, 1849).

https://doi.org/10.1515/9783111561547-008

> **About *Vanity Fair***
> William Makepeace Thackeray (1811–1863) is perhaps best described as a satirist who turned to the novel as the vehicle for his social commentary. His 1848 novel *Vanity Fair* was published serially in *Punch* (a leading periodical of the century) from January 1847 to July 1848, meaning readers would encounter only a few chapters of the work at a time and would need to purchase the next month's issue to read more: Dickens, famously, published in this way, as did many other authors of the period. At times affecting but largely amusing, *Vanity Fair*, subtitled *A Novel Without a Hero*, is styled as a puppet show put on by the narrator who guides the reader through the strange and at times bizarre world of the England of his day. The subtitle is perhaps very apropos: although characters like Amelia Sedley and George Osborne might have been heroes in another author's novel, it is the villainous and cunning Becky Sharp who lingers with the reader, watching her successes and failures in social situations with a perverse interest. Worth noting, too, is that Thackeray's narrator is as much a character as those in the world of the story: his voice, digressions, and commentary make up much of the bulk of *Vanity Fair*, and he treats his puppets with the detached glee of a master storyteller who knows precisely how to manipulate them to yield the best results.
>
> *Now on the novel . . .*

Before the Curtain

As the manager of the Performance sits before the curtain on the boards and looks into the Fair, a feeling of profound melancholy comes over him in his survey of the bustling place. There is a great quantity of eating and drinking, making love and jilting, laughing and the contrary, smoking, cheating, fighting, dancing and fiddling; there are bullies pushing about, bucks ogling the women, knaves picking pockets, policemen on the look-out, quacks (other quacks, plague take them!) bawling in front of their booths, and yokels looking up at the tinselled dancers and poor old rouged tumblers, while the light-fingered folk are operating upon their pockets behind. Yes, this is VANITY FAIR; not a moral place certainly; nor a merry one, though very noisy. Look at the faces of the actors and buffoons when they come off from their business; and Tom Fool washing the paint off his cheeks before he sits down to dinner with his wife and the little Jack Puddings behind the canvas. The curtain will be up presently, and he will be turning over head and heels, and crying, "How are you?"

A man with a reflective turn of mind, walking through an exhibition of this sort, will not be oppressed, I take it, by his own or other people's hilarity. An episode of humour or kindness touches and amuses him here and there – a pretty child looking at a gingerbread stall; a pretty girl blushing whilst her lover talks to her and chooses her fairing; poor Tom Fool, yonder behind the waggon, mumbling his bone with the honest family which lives by his tumbling; but the general impression is one more melancholy than mirthful. When you come home you sit down in a sober, contemplative, not uncharitable frame of mind, and apply yourself to your books or your business.

I have no other moral than this to tag to the present story of "Vanity Fair." Some people consider Fairs immoral altogether, and eschew such, with their servants and families: very likely they are right. But persons who think otherwise, and are of a lazy, or a benevolent, or a sarcastic mood, may perhaps like to step in for half an hour, and look at the performances. There are scenes of all sorts; some dreadful combats, some grand and lofty horse-riding, some scenes of high life, and some of very middling indeed; some love-making for the sentimental, and some light comic business; the whole accompanied by appropriate scenery and brilliantly illuminated with the Author's own candles.

What more has the Manager of the Performance to say? – To acknowledge the kindness with which it has been received in all the principal towns of England through which the Show has passed, and where it has been most favourably noticed by the respected conductors of the public Press, and by the Nobility and Gentry. He is proud to think that his Puppets have given satisfaction to the very best company in this empire. The famous little Becky Puppet has been pronounced to be uncommonly flexible in the joints, and lively on the wire; the Amelia Doll, though it has had a smaller circle of admirers, has yet been carved and dressed with the greatest care by the artist; the Dobbin Figure, though apparently clumsy, yet dances in a very amusing and natural manner; the Little Boys' Dance has been liked by some; and please to remark the richly dressed figure of the Wicked Nobleman, on which no expense has been spared, and which Old Nick will fetch away at the end of this singular performance.

And with this, and a profound bow to his patrons, the Manager retires, and the curtain rises.

LONDON, June 28, 1848

Chapter I

Chiswick Mall

While the present century was in its teens, and on one sunshiny morning in June, there drove up to the great iron gate of Miss Pinkerton's academy for young ladies, on Chiswick Mall, a large family coach, with two fat horses in blazing harness, driven by a fat coachman in a three-cornered hat and wig, at the rate of four miles an hour. A black servant, who reposed on the box beside the fat coachman, uncurled his bandy legs as soon as the equipage drew up opposite Miss Pinkerton's shining brass plate, and as he pulled the bell at least a score of young heads were seen peering out of the narrow windows of the stately old brick house. Nay, the acute observer might have recognized the little red nose of good-natured Miss Jemima Pinkerton herself, rising over some geranium pots in the window of that lady's own drawing-room.

"It is Mrs. Sedley's coach, sister," said Miss Jemima. "Sambo, the black servant, has just rung the bell; and the coachman has a new red waistcoat."

"Have you completed all the necessary preparations incident to Miss Sedley's departure, Miss Jemima?" asked Miss Pinkerton herself, that majestic lady; the Semiramis of Hammersmith, the friend of Doctor Johnson, the correspondent of Mrs. Chapone herself.

"The girls were up at four this morning, packing her trunks, sister," replied Miss Jemima; "we have made her a bow-pot."

"Say a bouquet, sister Jemima, 'tis more genteel."

"Well, a booky as big almost as a haystack; I have put up two bottles of the gillyflower water for Mrs. Sedley, and the receipt for making it, in Amelia's box."

"And I trust, Miss Jemima, you have made a copy of Miss Sedley's account. This is it, is it? Very good – ninety-three pounds, four shillings. Be kind enough to address it to John Sedley, Esquire, and to seal this billet which I have written to his lady."

In Miss Jemima's eyes an autograph letter of her sister, Miss Pinkerton, was an object of as deep veneration as would have been a letter from a sovereign. Only when her pupils quitted the establishment, or when they were about to be married, and once, when poor Miss Birch died of the scarlet fever, was Miss Pinkerton known to write personally to the parents of her pupils; and it was Jemima's opinion that if anything could console Mrs. Birch for her daughter's loss, it would be that pious and eloquent composition in which Miss Pinkerton announced the event.

In the present instance Miss Pinkerton's "billet" was to the following effect: –

The Mall, Chiswick, June 15, 18

MADAM, – After her six years' residence at the Mall, I have the honour and happiness of presenting Miss Amelia Sedley to her parents, as a young lady not unworthy to occupy a fitting position in their polished and refined circle. Those virtues which characterize the young English gentlewoman, those accomplishments which become her birth and station, will not be found wanting in the amiable Miss Sedley, whose INDUSTRY and OBEDIENCE have endeared her to her instructors, and whose delightful sweetness of temper has charmed her AGED and her YOUTHFUL companions.

In music, in dancing, in orthography, in every variety of embroidery and needlework, she will be found to have realized her friends' fondest wishes. In geography there is still much to be desired; and a careful and undeviating use of the backboard, for four hours daily during the next three years, is recommended as necessary to the acquirement of that dignified DEPORTMENT AND CARRIAGE, so requisite for every young lady of FASHION.

In the principles of religion and morality, Miss Sedley will be found worthy of an establishment which has been honoured by the presence of THE GREAT LEXICOGRAPHER, and the patronage of the admirable Mrs. Chapone. In leaving the Mall, Miss Amelia carries with her the hearts of her companions, and the affectionate regards of her mistress, who has the honour to subscribe herself,

Madam, Your most obliged humble servant, BARBARA PINKERTON

P.S. – Miss Sharp accompanies Miss Sedley. It is particularly requested that Miss Sharp's stay in Russell Square may not exceed ten days. The family of distinction with whom she is engaged, desire to avail themselves of her services as soon as possible.

This letter completed, Miss Pinkerton proceeded to write her own name, and Miss Sedley's, in the fly-leaf of a Johnson's Dictionary – the interesting work which she invariably presented to her scholars, on their departure from the Mall. On the cover was inserted a copy of "Lines addressed to a young lady on quitting Miss Pinkerton's school, at the Mall; by the late revered Doctor Samuel Johnson." In fact, the Lexicographer's name was always on the lips of this majestic woman, and a visit he had paid to her was the cause of her reputation and her fortune.

Being commanded by her elder sister to get "the Dictionary" from the cupboard, Miss Jemima had extracted two copies of the book from the receptacle in question. When Miss Pinkerton had finished the inscription in the first, Jemima, with rather a dubious and timid air, handed her the second.

"For whom is this, Miss Jemima?" said Miss Pinkerton, with awful coldness.

"For Becky Sharp," answered Jemima, trembling very much, and blushing over her withered face and neck, as she turned her back on her sister. "For Becky Sharp: she's going too."

"MISS JEMIMA!" exclaimed Miss Pinkerton, in the largest capitals. "Are you in your senses? Replace the Dixonary in the closet, and never venture to take such a liberty in future."

"Well, sister, it's only two-and-ninepence, and poor Becky will be miserable if she don't get one."

"Send Miss Sedley instantly to me," said Miss Pinkerton. And so venturing not to say another word, poor Jemima trotted off, exceedingly flurried and nervous.

Miss Sedley's papa was a merchant in London, and a man of some wealth; whereas Miss Sharp was an articled pupil, for whom Miss Pinkerton had done, as she thought, quite enough, without conferring upon her at parting the high honour of the Dixonary.

Although schoolmistresses' letters are to be trusted no more nor less than churchyard epitaphs; yet, as it sometimes happens that a person departs this life who is really deserving of all the praises the stone cutter carves over his bones; who IS a good Christian, a good parent, child, wife, or husband; who actually

DOES leave a disconsolate family to mourn his loss; so in academies of the male and female sex it occurs every now and then that the pupil is fully worthy of the praises bestowed by the disinterested instructor. Now, Miss Amelia Sedley was a young lady of this singular species; and deserved not only all that Miss Pinkerton said in her praise, but had many charming qualities which that pompous old Minerva of a woman could not see, from the differences of rank and age between her pupil and herself.

For she could not only sing like a lark, or a Mrs. Billington, and dance like Hillisberg or Parisot; and embroider beautifully; and spell as well as a Dixonary itself; but she had such a kindly, smiling, tender, gentle, generous heart of her own, as won the love of everybody who came near her, from Minerva herself down to the poor girl in the scullery, and the one-eyed tart-woman's daughter, who was permitted to vend her wares once a week to the young ladies in the Mall. She had twelve intimate and bosom friends out of the twenty-four young ladies. Even envious Miss Briggs never spoke ill of her; high and mighty Miss Saltire (Lord Dexter's granddaughter) allowed that her figure was genteel; and as for Miss Swartz, the rich woolly-haired mulatto from St. Kitt's, on the day Amelia went away, she was in such a passion of tears that they were obliged to send for Dr. Floss, and half tipsify her with salvolatile. Miss Pinkerton's attachment was, as may be supposed from the high position and eminent virtues of that lady, calm and dignified; but Miss Jemima had already whimpered several times at the idea of Amelia's departure; and, but for fear of her sister, would have gone off in downright hysterics, like the heiress (who paid double) of St. Kitt's. Such luxury of grief, however, is only allowed to parlour-boarders. Honest Jemima had all the bills, and the washing, and the mending, and the puddings, and the plate and crockery, and the servants to superintend. But why speak about her? It is probable that we shall not hear of her again from this moment to the end of time, and that when the great filigree iron gates are once closed on her, she and her awful sister will never issue therefrom into this little world of history.

But as we are to see a great deal of Amelia, there is no harm in saying, at the outset of our acquaintance, that she was a dear little creature; and a great mercy it is, both in life and in novels, which (and the latter especially) abound in villains of the most sombre sort, that we are to have for a constant companion so guileless and good-natured a person. As she is not a heroine, there is no need to describe her person; indeed I am afraid that her nose was rather short than otherwise, and her cheeks a great deal too round and red for a heroine; but her face blushed with rosy health, and her lips with the freshest of smiles, and she had a pair of eyes which sparkled with the brightest and honestest good-humour, except indeed when they filled with tears, and that was a great deal too often; for the silly thing would cry over a dead canary-bird; or over a mouse, that the cat haply had seized upon; or over the end of a novel, were it ever so stupid; and as for saying an unkind word to her, were any persons hard-hearted enough to do so – why, so much the worse for them. Even Miss Pinkerton, that austere and godlike woman, ceased scolding her after the first time, and though she no more comprehended sensibility than she did Algebra, gave all masters and teachers particular orders to treat Miss Sedley with the utmost gentleness, as harsh treatment was injurious to her.

So that when the day of departure came, between her two customs of laughing and crying, Miss Sedley was greatly puzzled how to act. She was glad to go home, and yet most woefully sad at leaving school. For three days before, little Laura Martin, the orphan, followed her about like a little dog. She had to make and receive at least fourteen presents – to make fourteen solemn promises of writing every week: "Send my letters under cover to my grandpapa, the Earl of Dexter," said Miss Saltire (who, by the way, was rather shabby). "Never mind the postage, but write every day, you dear darling," said the impetuous and woolly-headed, but generous and affectionate Miss Swartz; and the orphan little Laura Martin (who was just in round-hand), took her friend's hand and said, looking up in her face wistfully, "Amelia, when I write to you I shall call you Mamma." All which details, I have no doubt, JONES, who reads this book at his Club, will pronounce to be excessively foolish, trivial, twaddling, and ultra-sentimental. Yes; I can see Jones at this minute (rather flushed with his joint of mutton and half pint of wine), taking out his pencil and scoring under the words "foolish, twaddling," &c., and adding to them his own remark of "QUITE TRUE." Well, he is a lofty man of genius, and admires the great and heroic in life and novels; and so had better take warning and go elsewhere.

Well, then. The flowers, and the presents, and the trunks, and bonnet-boxes of Miss Sedley having been arranged by Mr. Sambo in the carriage, together with a very small and weather-beaten old cow's-skin trunk with Miss Sharp's card neatly nailed upon it, which was delivered by Sambo with a grin, and packed by the coachman with a corresponding sneer – the hour for parting came; and the grief of that moment was considerably lessened by the admirable discourse which Miss Pinkerton addressed to her pupil. Not that the parting speech caused Amelia to philosophise, or that it armed her in any way with a calmness, the result of argument; but it was intolerably dull, pompous, and tedious; and having the fear of her schoolmistress greatly before her eyes, Miss Sedley did not venture, in her presence, to give way to any ebullitions of private grief. A seed-cake and a bottle of wine were produced in the drawing-room, as on the solemn occasions of the visits of parents, and these refreshments being partaken of, Miss Sedley was at liberty to depart.

"You'll go in and say good-by to Miss Pinkerton, Becky!" said Miss Jemima to a young lady of whom nobody took any notice, and who was coming downstairs with her own bandbox.

"I suppose I must," said Miss Sharp calmly, and much to the wonder of Miss Jemima; and the latter having knocked at the door, and receiving permission to come in, Miss Sharp advanced in a very unconcerned manner, and said in French, and with a perfect accent, "Mademoiselle, je viens vous faire mes adieux."

Miss Pinkerton did not understand French; she only directed those who did: but biting her lips and throwing up her venerable and Roman-nosed head (on the top of which figured a large and solemn turban), she said, "Miss Sharp, I wish you a good morning." As the Hammersmith Semiramis spoke, she waved one hand, both by way of adieu, and to give Miss Sharp an opportunity of shaking one of the fingers of the hand which was left out for that purpose.

Miss Sharp only folded her own hands with a very frigid smile and bow, and quite declined to accept the proffered honour; on which Semiramis tossed up her turban more indignantly than ever. In fact, it was a little battle between the young lady and the old one, and the latter was worsted. "Heaven bless you, my child," said she, embracing Amelia, and scowling the while over the girl's shoulder at Miss Sharp. "Come away, Becky," said Miss Jemima, pulling the young woman away in great alarm, and the drawing-room door closed upon them for ever.

Then came the struggle and parting below. Words refuse to tell it. All the servants were there in the hall – all the dear friends – all the young ladies – the dancing-master who had just arrived; and there was such a scuffling, and hugging, and kissing, and crying, with the hysterical YOOPS of Miss Swartz, the parlour-boarder, from her room, as no pen can depict, and as the tender heart would fain pass over. The embracing was over; they parted – that is, Miss Sedley parted from her friends. Miss Sharp had demurely entered the carriage some minutes before. Nobody cried for leaving HER.

Sambo of the bandy legs slammed the carriage door on his young weeping mistress. He sprang up behind the carriage. "Stop!" cried Miss Jemima, rushing to the gate with a parcel.

"It's some sandwiches, my dear," said she to Amelia. "You may be hungry, you know; and Becky, Becky Sharp, here's a book for you that my sister – that is, I – Johnson's Dixonary, you know; you mustn't leave us without that. Good-by. Drive on, coachman. God bless you!"

And the kind creature retreated into the garden, overcome with emotion.

But, lo! and just as the coach drove off, Miss Sharp put her pale face out of the window and actually flung the book back into the garden.

This almost caused Jemima to faint with terror. "Well, I never" – said she – "what an audacious" – Emotion prevented her from completing either sentence. The carriage rolled away; the great gates were closed; the bell rang for the dancing lesson. The world is before the two young ladies; and so, farewell to Chiswick Mall.

Charles Dickens' *David Copperfield*

Published in 1849 in London. Available on Project Gutenberg at https://www.gutenberg.org/ebooks/766/ [last access 27.11.2024].

Image 9: Frontispiece in Charles Dickens, *David Copperfield*, 2 vols. (Philadelphia: T.B. Peterson, 1850).

About *David Copperfield*
Certainly one of the most famous and prolific authors in English history, Charles Dickens (1812–1870) is known for his melodramatic style, concern for the poor and disenfranchised, extremely lengthy novels, and often somewhat absurd plots. In *Bleak House*, for instance, a character spontaneously combusts; in *David Copperfield*, happenstance and random chance drive much of the

action, focalized through David himself, who writes the story of his life from the position of maturity and financial security. The novel was published serially from May 1849 to November 1850, and as a complete book in 1850. Like *Jane Eyre*, it is a coming-of-age novel, and also like *Jane Eyre*, its protagonist is soon made an orphan, turning to extended family and a network of friends to support his growth and education. Dickens' melodrama is on display throughout the text. Readers will laugh and cry with David, and the novel is best read without cynicism or irony: this is Dickens at his most Dickensian, and each emotion felt by characters and readers is powerful and blunt. David's grief is matched only by his triumphs, and the unusual cast of eccentric characters who surround him provide much of the fun in reading the novel.

Now to the novel . . .

Chapter I

I Am Born

Whether I shall turn out to be the hero of my own life, or whether that station will be held by anybody else, these pages must show. To begin my life with the beginning of my life, I record that I was born (as I have been informed and believe) on a Friday, at twelve o'clock at night. It was remarked that the clock began to strike, and I began to cry, simultaneously.

In consideration of the day and hour of my birth, it was declared by the nurse, and by some sage women in the neighbourhood who had taken a lively interest in me several months before there was any possibility of our becoming personally acquainted, first, that I was destined to be unlucky in life; and secondly, that I was privileged to see ghosts and spirits; both these gifts inevitably attaching, as they believed, to all unlucky infants of either gender, born towards the small hours on a Friday night.

I need say nothing here, on the first head, because nothing can show better than my history whether that prediction was verified or falsified by the result. On the second branch of the question, I will only remark, that unless I ran through that part of my inheritance while I was still a baby, I have not come into it yet. But I do not at all complain of having been kept out of this property; and if anybody else should be in the present enjoyment of it, he is heartily welcome to keep it.

I was born with a caul, which was advertised for sale, in the newspapers, at the low price of fifteen guineas. Whether sea-going people were short of money about that time, or were short of faith and preferred cork jackets, I don't know; all I know is, that there was but one solitary bidding, and that was from an attorney connected with the bill-broking business, who offered two pounds in cash, and the balance in sherry, but declined to be guaranteed from drowning on any higher bargain. Consequently the advertisement was withdrawn at a dead loss – for as to sherry, my poor dear mother's own sherry was in the market then – and ten years afterwards, the caul was put up in a raffle down in our part of the country, to fifty members at half-a-crown a head, the winner to spend five shillings. I was present myself, and I remember to have felt quite uncomfortable and confused, at a part of myself being disposed of in that way. The caul was won, I recollect, by an old lady with a hand-basket, who, very reluctantly, produced from it the stipulated five shillings, all in halfpence, and twopence halfpenny short – as it took an immense time and a great waste of arithmetic, to endeavour without any effect to prove to her. It is a fact which will be long remembered as remarkable down there, that she was never drowned, but died triumphantly in bed, at ninety-two. I have understood that it was, to the last, her proudest boast, that she never had been on the water in her life, except upon a bridge; and that over her tea (to which she was extremely partial) she, to the last, expressed her indignation at the impiety of mariners and others, who had the presumption to go 'meandering' about the world. It was in vain to represent to her that some conveniences, tea perhaps included, resulted from this objectionable practice. She always returned, with greater emphasis and with an instinctive knowledge of the strength of her objection, 'Let us have no meandering.'

Not to meander myself, at present, I will go back to my birth.

I was born at Blunderstone, in Suffolk, or 'there by', as they say in Scotland. I was a posthumous child. My father's eyes had closed upon the light of this world six months, when mine opened on it. There is something strange to me, even now, in the reflection that he never saw me; and something stranger yet in the shadowy remembrance that I have of my first childish associations with his white grave-stone in the churchyard, and of the indefinable compassion I used to feel for it lying out alone there in the dark night, when our little parlour was warm and bright with fire and candle, and the doors of our house were – almost cruelly, it seemed to me sometimes – bolted and locked against it.

An aunt of my father's, and consequently a great-aunt of mine, of whom I shall have more to relate by and by, was the principal magnate of our family. Miss Trotwood, or Miss Betsey, as my poor mother always called her, when she sufficiently overcame her dread of this formidable personage to mention her at all (which was seldom), had been married to a husband younger than herself, who was very handsome, except in the sense of the homely adage, 'handsome is, that handsome does' – for he was strongly suspected of having beaten Miss Betsey, and even of having once, on a disputed question of supplies, made some hasty but determined arrangements to throw her out of a two pair of stairs' window. These evidences of an incompatibility of temper induced Miss Betsey to pay him off, and effect a separation by mutual consent. He went to India with his capital, and there, according to a wild legend in our family, he was once seen riding on an elephant, in company with a Baboon; but I think it must have been a Baboo – or a Begum. Anyhow, from India tidings of his death reached home, within ten years. How they affected my aunt, nobody knew; for immediately upon the separation, she took her maiden name again, bought a cottage in a hamlet on the sea-coast a long way off, established herself there as a single woman with one servant, and was understood to live secluded, ever afterwards, in an inflexible retirement.

My father had once been a favourite of hers, I believe; but she was mortally affronted by his marriage, on the ground that my mother was 'a wax doll'. She had never seen my mother, but she knew her to be not yet twenty. My father and Miss Betsey never met again. He was double my mother's age when he married, and of but a delicate constitution. He died a year afterwards, and, as I have said, six months before I came into the world.

This was the state of matters, on the afternoon of, what I may be excused for calling, that eventful and important Friday. I can make no claim therefore to have known, at that time, how matters stood; or to have any remembrance, founded on the evidence of my own senses, of what follows.

My mother was sitting by the fire, but poorly in health, and very low in spirits, looking at it through her tears, and desponding heavily about herself and the fatherless little stranger, who was already welcomed by some grosses of prophetic pins, in a drawer upstairs, to a world not at all excited on the subject of his arrival; my mother, I say, was sitting by the fire, that bright, windy March afternoon, very timid and sad, and very doubtful of ever coming alive out of the trial that was before her, when, lifting her eyes as she dried them, to the window opposite, she saw a strange lady coming up the garden.

My mother had a sure foreboding at the second glance, that it was Miss Betsey. The setting sun was glowing on the strange lady, over the garden-fence, and she came walking up to the door with a fell rigidity of figure and composure of countenance that could have belonged to nobody else.

When she reached the house, she gave another proof of her identity. My father had often hinted that she seldom conducted herself like any ordinary Christian; and now, instead of ringing the bell, she came and looked in at that identical window, pressing the end of her nose against the glass to that extent, that my poor dear mother used to say it became perfectly flat and white in a moment.

She gave my mother such a turn, that I have always been convinced I am indebted to Miss Betsey for having been born on a Friday.

My mother had left her chair in her agitation, and gone behind it in the corner. Miss Betsey, looking round the room, slowly and inquiringly, began on the other side, and carried her eyes on, like a Saracen's Head in a Dutch clock, until they reached my mother. Then she made a frown and a gesture to my mother, like one who was accustomed to be obeyed, to come and open the door. My mother went.

'Mrs. David Copperfield, I think,' said Miss Betsey; the emphasis referring, perhaps, to my mother's mourning weeds, and her condition.

'Yes,' said my mother, faintly.

'Miss Trotwood,' said the visitor. 'You have heard of her, I dare say?'

My mother answered she had had that pleasure. And she had a disagreeable consciousness of not appearing to imply that it had been an overpowering pleasure.

'Now you see her,' said Miss Betsey. My mother bent her head, and begged her to walk in.

They went into the parlour my mother had come from, the fire in the best room on the other side of the passage not being lighted – not having been lighted, indeed, since my father's funeral; and when they were both seated, and Miss Betsey said nothing, my mother, after vainly trying to restrain herself, began to cry. 'Oh tut, tut, tut!' said Miss Betsey, in a hurry. 'Don't do that! Come, come!'

My mother couldn't help it notwithstanding, so she cried until she had had her cry out.

'Take off your cap, child,' said Miss Betsey, 'and let me see you.'

My mother was too much afraid of her to refuse compliance with this odd request, if she had any disposition to do so. Therefore she did as she was told, and did it with such nervous hands that her hair (which was luxuriant and beautiful) fell all about her face.

'Why, bless my heart!' exclaimed Miss Betsey. 'You are a very Baby!'

My mother was, no doubt, unusually youthful in appearance even for her years; she hung her head, as if it were her fault, poor thing, and said, sobbing, that indeed she was afraid she was but a childish widow, and would be but a childish mother if she lived. In a short pause which ensued, she had a fancy that she felt Miss Betsey touch her hair, and that with no ungentle hand; but, looking at her, in her timid hope, she found that lady sitting with the skirt of her dress tucked up, her hands folded on one knee, and her feet upon the fender, frowning at the fire.

'In the name of Heaven,' said Miss Betsey, suddenly, 'why Rookery?'

'Do you mean the house, ma'am?' asked my mother.

'Why Rookery?' said Miss Betsey. 'Cookery would have been more to the purpose, if you had had any practical ideas of life, either of you.'

'The name was Mr. Copperfield's choice,' returned my mother. 'When he bought the house, he liked to think that there were rooks about it.'

The evening wind made such a disturbance just now, among some tall old elm-trees at the bottom of the garden, that neither my mother nor Miss Betsey could forbear glancing that way. As the elms bent to one another, like giants who were whispering secrets, and after a few seconds of such repose, fell into a violent flurry, tossing their wild arms about, as if their late confidences were really too wicked for their peace of mind, some weatherbeaten ragged old rooks'-nests, burdening their higher branches, swung like wrecks upon a stormy sea.

'Where are the birds?' asked Miss Betsey.

'The – ?' My mother had been thinking of something else.

'The rooks – what has become of them?' asked Miss Betsey.

'There have not been any since we have lived here,' said my mother. 'We thought – Mr. Copperfield thought – it was quite a large rookery; but the nests were very old ones, and the birds have deserted them a long while.'

'David Copperfield all over!' cried Miss Betsey. 'David Copperfield from head to foot! Calls a house a rookery when there's not a rook near it, and takes the birds on trust, because he sees the nests!'

'Mr. Copperfield,' returned my mother, 'is dead, and if you dare to speak unkindly of him to me – '

My poor dear mother, I suppose, had some momentary intention of committing an assault and battery upon my aunt, who could easily have settled her with one hand, even if my mother had been in far better training for such an encounter than she was that evening. But it passed with the action of rising from her chair; and she sat down again very meekly, and fainted.

When she came to herself, or when Miss Betsey had restored her, whichever it was, she found the latter standing at the window. The twilight was by this time shading down into darkness; and dimly as they saw each other, they could not have done that without the aid of the fire.

'Well?' said Miss Betsey, coming back to her chair, as if she had only been taking a casual look at the prospect; 'and when do you expect – '

'I am all in a tremble,' faltered my mother. 'I don't know what's the matter. I shall die, I am sure!'

'No, no, no,' said Miss Betsey. 'Have some tea.'

'Oh dear me, dear me, do you think it will do me any good?' cried my mother in a helpless manner.

'Of course it will,' said Miss Betsey. 'It's nothing but fancy. What do you call your girl?'

'I don't know that it will be a girl, yet, ma'am,' said my mother innocently.

'Bless the Baby!' exclaimed Miss Betsey, unconsciously quoting the second sentiment of the pincushion in the drawer upstairs, but applying it to my mother instead of me, 'I don't mean that. I mean your servant-girl.'

'Peggotty,' said my mother.

'Peggotty!' repeated Miss Betsey, with some indignation. 'Do you mean to say, child, that any human being has gone into a Christian church, and got herself named Peggotty?' 'It's her surname,' said my mother, faintly. 'Mr. Copperfield called her by it, because her Christian name was the same as mine.'

'Here! Peggotty!' cried Miss Betsey, opening the parlour door. 'Tea. Your mistress is a little unwell. Don't dawdle.'

Having issued this mandate with as much potentiality as if she had been a recognized authority in the house ever since it had been a house, and having looked out to confront the amazed Peggotty coming along the passage with a candle at the sound of a strange voice, Miss Betsey shut the door again, and sat down as before: with her feet on the fender, the skirt of her dress tucked up, and her hands folded on one knee.

'You were speaking about its being a girl,' said Miss Betsey. 'I have no doubt it will be a girl. I have a presentiment that it must be a girl. Now child, from the moment of the birth of this girl – '

'Perhaps boy,' my mother took the liberty of putting in.

'I tell you I have a presentiment that it must be a girl,' returned Miss Betsey. 'Don't contradict. From the moment of this girl's birth, child, I intend to be her friend. I intend to be her godmother, and I beg you'll call her Betsey Trotwood Copperfield. There must be no mistakes in life with THIS Betsey Trotwood. There must be no trifling with HER affections, poor dear. She must be well brought up, and well guarded from reposing any foolish confidences where they are not deserved. I must make that MY care.'

There was a twitch of Miss Betsey's head, after each of these sentences, as if her own old wrongs were working within her, and she repressed any plainer reference to them by strong constraint. So my mother suspected, at least, as she observed her by the low glimmer of the fire: too much scared by Miss Betsey, too uneasy in herself, and too subdued and bewildered altogether, to observe anything very clearly, or to know what to say.

'And was David good to you, child?' asked Miss Betsey, when she had been silent for a little while, and these motions of her head had gradually ceased. 'Were you comfortable together?'

'We were very happy,' said my mother. 'Mr. Copperfield was only too good to me.'

'What, he spoilt you, I suppose?' returned Miss Betsey.

'For being quite alone and dependent on myself in this rough world again, yes, I fear he did indeed,' sobbed my mother.

'Well! Don't cry!' said Miss Betsey. 'You were not equally matched, child – if any two people can be equally matched – and so I asked the question. You were an orphan, weren't you?' 'Yes.'

'And a governess?'

'I was nursery-governess in a family where Mr. Copperfield came to visit. Mr. Copperfield was very kind to me, and took a great deal of notice of me, and paid me a good deal of attention, and at last proposed to me. And I accepted him. And so we were married,' said my mother simply.

'Ha! Poor Baby!' mused Miss Betsey, with her frown still bent upon the fire. 'Do you know anything?'

'I beg your pardon, ma'am,' faltered my mother.

'About keeping house, for instance,' said Miss Betsey.

'Not much, I fear,' returned my mother. 'Not so much as I could wish. But Mr. Copperfield was teaching me –'

('Much he knew about it himself!') said Miss Betsey in a parenthesis. – 'And I hope I should have improved, being very anxious to learn, and he very patient to teach me, if the great misfortune of his death' – my mother broke down again here, and could get no farther.

'Well, well!' said Miss Betsey. – 'I kept my housekeeping-book regularly, and balanced it with Mr. Copperfield every night,' cried my mother in another burst of distress, and breaking down again.

'Well, well!' said Miss Betsey. 'Don't cry any more.' – 'And I am sure we never had a word of difference respecting it, except when Mr. Copperfield objected to my threes and fives being too much like each other, or to my putting curly tails to my sevens and nines,' resumed my mother in another burst, and breaking down again.

'You'll make yourself ill,' said Miss Betsey, 'and you know that will not be good either for you or for my god-daughter. Come! You mustn't do it!'

This argument had some share in quieting my mother, though her increasing indisposition had a larger one. There was an interval of silence, only broken by Miss Betsey's occasionally ejaculating 'Ha!' as she sat with her feet upon the fender.

'David had bought an annuity for himself with his money, I know,' said she, by and by. 'What did he do for you?'

'Mr. Copperfield,' said my mother, answering with some difficulty, 'was so considerate and good as to secure the reversion of a part of it to me.'

'How much?' asked Miss Betsey.

'A hundred and five pounds a year,' said my mother.

'He might have done worse,' said my aunt.

The word was appropriate to the moment. My mother was so much worse that Peggotty, coming in with the teaboard and candles, and seeing at a glance how ill she was, – as Miss Betsey might have done sooner if there had been light enough, – conveyed her upstairs to her own room with all speed; and immediately dispatched Ham Peggotty, her nephew, who had been for some days past secreted in the house, unknown to my mother, as a special messenger in case of emergency, to fetch the nurse and doctor.

Those allied powers were considerably astonished, when they arrived within a few minutes of each other, to find an unknown lady of portentous appearance, sitting before the fire, with her bonnet tied over her left arm, stopping her ears with jewellers' cotton. Peggotty knowing nothing about her, and my mother saying nothing about her, she was quite a mystery in the parlour; and the fact of her having a magazine of jewellers' cotton in her pocket, and sticking the article in her ears in that way, did not detract from the solemnity of her presence.

The doctor having been upstairs and come down again, and having satisfied himself, I suppose, that there was a probability of this unknown lady and himself having to sit there, face to face, for some hours, laid himself out to be polite and social. He was the meekest of his sex, the mildest of little men. He sidled in and out of a room, to take up the less space. He walked as softly as the Ghost in Hamlet, and more slowly. He carried his head on one side, partly in modest depreciation of himself, partly in modest propitiation of everybody else. It is nothing to say that he hadn't a word to throw at a dog. He couldn't have thrown a word at a mad dog. He might have offered him one gently, or half a one, or a fragment of one; for he spoke as slowly as he walked; but he wouldn't have been rude to him, and he couldn't have been quick with him, for any earthly consideration.

Mr. Chillip, looking mildly at my aunt with his head on one side, and making her a little bow, said, in allusion to the jewellers' cotton, as he softly touched his left ear:

'Some local irritation, ma'am?'

'What!' replied my aunt, pulling the cotton out of one ear like a cork.

Mr. Chillip was so alarmed by her abruptness – as he told my mother afterwards – that it was a mercy he didn't lose his presence of mind. But he repeated sweetly:

'Some local irritation, ma'am?'

'Nonsense!' replied my aunt, and corked herself again, at one blow.

Mr. Chillip could do nothing after this, but sit and look at her feebly, as she sat and looked at the fire, until he was called upstairs again. After some quarter of an hour's absence, he returned.

'Well?' said my aunt, taking the cotton out of the ear nearest to him.

'Well, ma'am,' returned Mr. Chillip, 'we are – we are progressing slowly, ma'am.'

'Ba – a – ah!' said my aunt, with a perfect shake on the contemptuous interjection. And corked herself as before.

Really – really – as Mr. Chillip told my mother, he was almost shocked; speaking in a professional point of view alone, he was almost shocked. But he sat and looked at her, notwithstanding, for nearly two hours, as she sat looking at the fire, until he was again called out. After another absence, he again returned.

'Well?' said my aunt, taking out the cotton on that side again.

'Well, ma'am,' returned Mr. Chillip, 'we are – we are progressing slowly, ma'am.'

'Ya – a – ah!' said my aunt. With such a snarl at him, that Mr. Chillip absolutely could not bear it. It was really calculated to break his spirit, he said afterwards. He preferred to go and sit upon the stairs, in the dark and a strong draught, until he was again sent for.

Ham Peggotty, who went to the national school, and was a very dragon at his catechism, and who may therefore be regarded as a credible witness, reported next day, that happening to peep in at the parlour-door an hour after this, he was instantly descried by Miss Betsey, then walking to and fro in a state of agitation, and pounced upon before he could make his escape. That there were now occasional sounds of feet and voices overhead which he inferred the cotton did not exclude, from the circumstance of his evidently being clutched by the lady as a victim on whom to expend her superabundant agitation when the sounds were loudest. That, marching him constantly up and down by the collar (as if he had been taking too much laudanum), she, at those times, shook him, rumpled his hair, made light of his linen, stopped his ears as if she confounded them with her own, and otherwise tousled and maltreated him. This was in part confirmed by his aunt, who saw him at half past twelve o'clock, soon after his release, and affirmed that he was then as red as I was.

The mild Mr. Chillip could not possibly bear malice at such a time, if at any time. He sidled into the parlour as soon as he was at liberty, and said to my aunt in his meekest manner:

'Well, ma'am, I am happy to congratulate you.'

'What upon?' said my aunt, sharply.

Mr. Chillip was fluttered again, by the extreme severity of my aunt's manner; so he made her a little bow and gave her a little smile, to mollify her.

'Mercy on the man, what's he doing!' cried my aunt, impatiently. 'Can't he speak?'

'Be calm, my dear ma'am,' said Mr. Chillip, in his softest accents. 'There is no longer any occasion for uneasiness, ma'am. Be calm.'

It has since been considered almost a miracle that my aunt didn't shake him, and shake what he had to say, out of him. She only shook her own head at him, but in a way that made him quail.

'Well, ma'am,' resumed Mr. Chillip, as soon as he had courage, 'I am happy to congratulate you. All is now over, ma'am, and well over.'

During the five minutes or so that Mr. Chillip devoted to the delivery of this oration, my aunt eyed him narrowly.

'How is she?' said my aunt, folding her arms with her bonnet still tied on one of them.

'Well, ma'am, she will soon be quite comfortable, I hope,' returned Mr. Chillip. 'Quite as comfortable as we can expect a young mother to be, under these melancholy domestic circumstances. There cannot be any objection to your seeing her presently, ma'am. It may do her good.'

'And SHE. How is SHE?' said my aunt, sharply.

Mr. Chillip laid his head a little more on one side, and looked at my aunt like an amiable bird.

'The baby,' said my aunt. 'How is she?'

'Ma'am,' returned Mr. Chillip, 'I apprehended you had known. It's a boy.'

My aunt said never a word, but took her bonnet by the strings, in the manner of a sling, aimed a blow at Mr. Chillip's head with it, put it on bent, walked out, and never came back. She vanished like a discontented fairy; or like one of those supernatural beings, whom it was popularly supposed I was entitled to see; and never came back any more.

No. I lay in my basket, and my mother lay in her bed; but Betsey Trotwood Copperfield was for ever in the land of dreams and shadows, the tremendous region whence I had so lately travelled; and the light upon the window of our room shone out upon the earthly bourne of all such travellers, and the mound above the ashes and the dust that once was he, without whom I had never been.

Lewis Carroll's *Alice's Adventures in Wonderland*

Published in 1865 in London. Available on Project Gutenberg, at https://www.gutenberg.org/ebooks/11/ [last access 27.11.2024].

Image 10: John Tenniel, No. 25, 1864, illustration in *Alice in Wonderland*, by Lewis Carroll (Mount Vernon, NY: Peter Pauper press, 1940), 94.

About *Alice's Adventures in Wonderland*
Lewis Carroll, born 1832 as Charles Dodgson, was a novelist, poet, photographer, and mathematician. He was also, undoubtedly, a master of children's literature. The delightful *Alice's Adventures in Wonderland* includes extensive linguistic play, leaps in logic, and jokes and puns aimed at children and their parents alike. His writing is overwhelmingly playful: Carroll uses language as well as any author of his day, and knows precisely what sounds compelling – and funny – to the ear. Although the 1865 *Alice* and its 1871 sequel *Through the Looking-Glass and What Alice Found There* are ostensibly works written for children, there is much here for adult readers: the narrative logic at work, the transient, dreamy world Alice finds herself in, and her misadventures have at times been read as allegories for puberty, a deep look into the child psyche, and much more. It is up to the individual reader to determine how one might best understand Carroll's project, and, along the way, enjoy the fanciful wordplay, jokes, and knowing winks.

Now to the novel . . .

https://doi.org/10.1515/9783111561547-010

Chapter VII

A Mad Tea Party

There was a table set out under a tree in front of the house, and the March Hare and the Hatter were having tea at it: a Dormouse was sitting between them, fast asleep, and the other two were using it as a cushion, resting their elbows on it, and talking over its head. "Very uncomfortable for the Dormouse," thought Alice; "only, as it's asleep, I suppose it doesn't mind."

The table was a large one, but the three were all crowded together at one corner of it: "No room! No room!" they cried out when they saw Alice coming. "There's *plenty* of room!" said Alice indignantly, and she sat down in a large armchair at one end of the table.

"Have some wine," the March Hare said in an encouraging tone.

Alice looked all round the table, but there was nothing on it but tea. "I don't see any wine," she remarked.

"There isn't any," said the March Hare.

"Then it wasn't very civil of you to offer it," said Alice angrily.

"It wasn't very civil of you to sit down without being invited," said the March Hare.

"I didn't know it was *your* table," said Alice; "it's laid for a great many more than three."

"Your hair wants cutting," said the Hatter. He had been looking at Alice for some time with great curiosity, and this was his first speech.

"You should learn not to make personal remarks," Alice said with some severity; "it's very rude."

The Hatter opened his eyes very wide on hearing this; but all he *said* was, "Why is a raven like a writing-desk?"

"Come, we shall have some fun now!" thought Alice. "I'm glad they've begun asking riddles. – I believe I can guess that," she added aloud.

"Do you mean that you think you can find out the answer to it?" said the March Hare.

"Exactly so," said Alice.

"Then you should say what you mean," the March Hare went on.

"I do," Alice hastily replied; "at least – at least I mean what I say – that's the same thing, you know."

"Not the same thing a bit!" said the Hatter. "You might just as well say that 'I see what I eat' is the same thing as 'I eat what I see'!"

"You might just as well say," added the March Hare, "that 'I like what I get' is the same thing as 'I get what I like'!"

"You might just as well say," added the Dormouse, who seemed to be talking in his sleep, "that 'I breathe when I sleep' is the same thing as 'I sleep when I breathe'!"

"It *is* the same thing with you," said the Hatter, and here the conversation dropped, and the party sat silent for a minute, while Alice thought over all she could remember about ravens and writing-desks, which wasn't much.

The Hatter was the first to break the silence. "What day of the month is it?" he said, turning to Alice: he had taken his watch out of his pocket, and was looking at it uneasily, shaking it every now and then, and holding it to his ear.

Alice considered a little, and then said "The fourth."

"Two days wrong!" sighed the Hatter. "I told you butter wouldn't suit the works!" he added looking angrily at the March Hare.

"It was the *best* butter," the March Hare meekly replied.

"Yes, but some crumbs must have got in as well," the Hatter grumbled: "you shouldn't have put it in with the bread-knife."

The March Hare took the watch and looked at it gloomily: then he dipped it into his cup of tea, and looked at it again: but he could think of nothing better to say than his first remark, "It was the *best* butter, you know."

Alice had been looking over his shoulder with some curiosity. "What a funny watch!" she remarked. "It tells the day of the month, and doesn't tell what o'clock it is!"

"Why should it?" muttered the Hatter. "Does *your* watch tell you what year it is?"

"Of course not," Alice replied very readily: "but that's because it stays the same year for such a long time together."

"Which is just the case with *mine*," said the Hatter.

Alice felt dreadfully puzzled. The Hatter's remark seemed to have no sort of meaning in it, and yet it was certainly English. "I don't quite understand you," she said, as politely as she could.

"The Dormouse is asleep again," said the Hatter, and he poured a little hot tea upon its nose.

The Dormouse shook its head impatiently, and said, without opening its eyes, "Of course, of course; just what I was going to remark myself."

"Have you guessed the riddle yet?" the Hatter said, turning to Alice again.

"No, I give it up," Alice replied: "what's the answer?"

"I haven't the slightest idea," said the Hatter.

"Nor I," said the March Hare.

Alice sighed wearily. "I think you might do something better with the time," she said, "than waste it in asking riddles that have no answers."

"If you knew Time as well as I do," said the Hatter, "you wouldn't talk about wasting *it*. It's *him*."

"I don't know what you mean," said Alice.

"Of course you don't!" the Hatter said, tossing his head contemptuously. "I dare say you never even spoke to Time!"

"Perhaps not," Alice cautiously replied: "but I know I have to beat time when I learn music."

"Ah! that accounts for it," said the Hatter. "He won't stand beating. Now, if you only kept on good terms with him, he'd do almost anything you liked with the clock. For instance, suppose it were nine o'clock in the morning, just time to begin lessons: you'd only have to whisper a hint to Time, and round goes the clock in a twinkling! Half-past one, time for dinner!"

("I only wish it was," the March Hare said to itself in a whisper.)

"That would be grand, certainly," said Alice thoughtfully: "but then – I shouldn't be hungry for it, you know."

"Not at first, perhaps," said the Hatter: "but you could keep it to half-past one as long as you liked."

"Is that the way *you* manage?" Alice asked.

The Hatter shook his head mournfully. "Not I!" he replied. "We quarrelled last March – just before *he* went mad, you know –" (pointing with his tea spoon at the March Hare,) "– it was at the great concert given by the Queen of Hearts, and I had to sing

'Twinkle, twinkle, little bat!
How I wonder what you're at!'

You know the song, perhaps?"

"I've heard something like it," said Alice.

"It goes on, you know," the Hatter continued, "in this way: –

'Up above the world you fly,
Like a tea-tray in the sky.
Twinkle, twinkle –'"

Here the Dormouse shook itself, and began singing in its sleep "*Twinkle, twinkle, twinkle, twinkle –*" and went on so long that they had to pinch it to make it stop.

"Well, I'd hardly finished the first verse," said the Hatter, "when the Queen jumped up and bawled out, 'He's murdering the time! Off with his head!'"

"How dreadfully savage!" exclaimed Alice.

"And ever since that," the Hatter went on in a mournful tone, "he won't do a thing I ask! It's always six o'clock now."

A bright idea came into Alice's head. "Is that the reason so many tea-things are put out here?" she asked.

"Yes, that's it," said the Hatter with a sigh: "it's always tea-time, and we've no time to wash the things between whiles."

"Then you keep moving round, I suppose?" said Alice.

"Exactly so," said the Hatter: "as the things get used up."

"But what happens when you come to the beginning again?" Alice ventured to ask.

"Suppose we change the subject," the March Hare interrupted, yawning. "I'm getting tired of this. I vote the young lady tells us a story."

"I'm afraid I don't know one," said Alice, rather alarmed at the proposal.

"Then the Dormouse shall!" they both cried. "Wake up, Dormouse!" And they pinched it on both sides at once.

The Dormouse slowly opened his eyes. "I wasn't asleep," he said in a hoarse, feeble voice: "I heard every word you fellows were saying."

"Tell us a story!" said the March Hare.

"Yes, please do!" pleaded Alice.

"And be quick about it," added the Hatter, "or you'll be asleep again before it's done."

"Once upon a time there were three little sisters," the Dormouse began in a great hurry; "and their names were Elsie, Lacie, and Tillie; and they lived at the bottom of a well –"

"What did they live on?" said Alice, who always took a great interest in questions of eating and drinking.

"They lived on treacle," said the Dormouse, after thinking a minute or two.

"They couldn't have done that, you know," Alice gently remarked; "they'd have been ill."

"So they were," said the Dormouse; "*very* ill."

Alice tried to fancy to herself what such an extraordinary ways of living would be like, but it puzzled her too much, so she went on: "But why did they live at the bottom of a well?"

"Take some more tea," the March Hare said to Alice, very earnestly.

"I've had nothing yet," Alice replied in an offended tone, "so I can't take more."

"You mean you can't take *less*," said the Hatter: "it's very easy to take *more* than nothing."

"Nobody asked *your* opinion," said Alice.

"Who's making personal remarks now?" the Hatter asked triumphantly.

Alice did not quite know what to say to this: so she helped herself to some tea and bread-and-butter, and then turned to the Dormouse, and repeated her question. "Why did they live at the bottom of a well?"

The Dormouse again took a minute or two to think about it, and then said, "It was a treacle-well."

"There's no such thing!" Alice was beginning very angrily, but the Hatter and the March Hare went "Sh! sh!" and the Dormouse sulkily remarked, "If you can't be civil, you'd better finish the story for yourself."

"No, please go on!" Alice said very humbly; "I won't interrupt again. I dare say there may be *one*."

"One, indeed!" said the Dormouse indignantly. However, he consented to go on. "And so these three little sisters – they were learning to draw, you know –"

"What did they draw?" said Alice, quite forgetting her promise.

"Treacle," said the Dormouse, without considering at all this time.

"I want a clean cup," interrupted the Hatter: "let's all move one place on."

He moved on as he spoke, and the Dormouse followed him: the March Hare moved into the Dormouse's place, and Alice rather unwillingly took the place of the March Hare. The Hatter was the only one who got any advantage from the change: and Alice was a good deal worse off than before, as the March Hare had just upset the milk-jug into his plate.

Alice did not wish to offend the Dormouse again, so she began very cautiously: "But I don't understand. Where did they draw the treacle from?"

"You can draw water out of a water-well," said the Hatter; "so I should think you could draw treacle out of a treacle-well – eh, stupid?"

"But they were *in* the well," Alice said to the Dormouse, not choosing to notice this last remark.

"Of course they were," said the Dormouse; "– well in."

This answer so confused poor Alice, that she let the Dormouse go on for some time without interrupting it.

"They were learning to draw," the Dormouse went on, yawning and rubbing its eyes, for it was getting very sleepy; "and they drew all manner of things – everything that begins with an M –"

"Why with an M?" said Alice.

"Why not?" said the March Hare.

Alice was silent.

The Dormouse had closed its eyes by this time, and was going off into a doze; but, on being pinched by the Hatter, it woke up again with a little shriek, and went on: "– that begins with an M, such as mouse-traps, and the moon, and memory, and muchness – you know you say things are "much of a muchness" – did you ever see such a thing as a drawing of a muchness?"

"Really, now you ask me," said Alice, very much confused, "I don't think –"

"Then you shouldn't talk," said the Hatter.

This piece of rudeness was more than Alice could bear: she got up in great disgust, and walked off; the Dormouse fell asleep instantly, and neither of the others took the least notice of her going, though she looked back once or twice, half hoping that they would call after her: the last time she saw them, they were trying to put the Dormouse into the teapot.

"At any rate I'll never go *there* again!" said Alice as she picked her way through the wood. "It's the stupidest tea-party I ever was at in all my life!"

Just as she said this, she noticed that one of the trees had a door leading right into it. "That's very curious!" she thought. "But everything's curious today. I think I may as well go in at once." And in she went.

Once more she found herself in the long hall, and close to the little glass table. "Now, I'll manage better this time," she said to herself, and began by taking the little golden key, and unlocking the door that led into the garden. Then she went to work nibbling at the mushroom (she had kept a piece of it in her pocket) till she was about a foot high: then she walked down the little passage: and *then* – she found herself at last in the beautiful garden, among the bright flower-beds and the cool fountains.

Additional Novels

Brontë, Emily. *Wuthering Heights*. London, 1847. Project Gutenberg, https://www.gutenberg.org/ebooks/768/ [last access 27.11.2024].
Dickens, Charles. *Bleak House*. London, 1852. Project Gutenberg, https://www.gutenberg.org/ebooks/1023/ [last access 27.11.2024].
Gaskell, Elizabeth. *North and South*. London, 1854. Project Gutenberg, https://www.gutenberg.org/ebooks/4276/ [last access 27.11.2024].
Barrett Browning, Elizabeth. *Aurora Leigh*. London, 1857. Project Gutenberg, https://www.gutenberg.org/ebooks/56621/ [last access 27.11.2024].
Trollope, Anthony. *Barchester Towers*. London, 1857. Project Gutenberg, https://www.gutenberg.org/ebooks/3409/ [last access 27.11.2024].
Dickens, Charles. *Great Expectations*. London, 1860. Project Gutenberg, https://www.gutenberg.org/ebooks/1400/ [last access 27.11.2024].
Eliot, George. *The Mill on the Floss*. London, 1860. Project Gutenberg, https://www.gutenberg.org/ebooks/6688/ [last access 27.11.2024].
Braddon, Mary Elizabeth. *Lady Audley's Secret*. London, 1862. Project Gutenberg, https://www.gutenberg.org/ebooks/8954/ [last access 27.11.2024].
Collins, Wilkie. *The Moonstone*. London, 1868. Project Gutenberg, https://www.gutenberg.org/ebooks/155/ [last access 27.11.2024].

Late Victorian Novels

Image 11: John O'Connor, "The Embankment, London," 1874.

As the century drew to a close, the sense that an era was truly ending hung heavy in the London air. Generations of Victorians had grown up and grown old with their queen, and now had to ask, what did it mean to be Victorian? Perhaps more to the point: what would come after the Victorians, and how would the Victorians be looked upon once their era was over? The wars were beginning to compound, and, while the British Empire would remain powerful for decades to come, the endless expansion of territory and accumulation of power was beginning to reach its limit. The fin de siècle anxiety manifested in literature which grew plodding in its plotting and as decadent as it was contemplative. Perhaps the finest novel of the nineteenth century – *Middlemarch* – was famously called by Virginia Woolf "one of the few English novels written for grownup people"; compare its grounded and robust psychic landscapes of everyday people to the fantastical visions of the unknown in *Dracula* and *The Time Machine*.

The boundless potential of the mid-century gave way, slowly but surely, to two literary phenomena in Naturalism and the Decadent movement, both of which reject the steady upward climb seen in the coming-of-age novels of the 1840s and 50s. Whether attempting to stave off the inevitable forward march of time or rage against the end of their epoch, the novelists of the late-century embraced the sordid and cruel underbelly that the novel as a genre had the ability to represent, but which had so typically been drenched and sanitized in melodrama decades earlier. The death of Victoria in 1901 was the end of an era, of course, but the slow, encroaching malaise of the final years of her reign runs deep in the novels of the period.

George Eliot's *Middlemarch*

Printed in 1871 in London. Available on Project Gutenberg, at https://www.gutenberg.org/ebooks/145/ [last access 27.11.2024].

Image 12: Jessica Landseer, "Village Scene," 1817.

About *Middlemarch*
George Eliot (1819–1880) is one of the undisputed masters of the novel as a genre, and her novel *Middlemarch* remains one of the finest novels ever written. Inspired, as the story goes, by tidepools containing small maritime animals that Eliot saw on a beach, the novel has been described by Virginia Woolf as "one of the few English novels written for grown-up people." Its winding plots between a massive cast of characters who are almost all much more than they first appear may initially be intimidating and difficult to keep track of, but, like the novel's substantial length, this is a hurdle that the reader must overcome to get to the heart of Eliot's literary project. Published in 1871–1872, the novel is set forty years prior, as Eliot's readers were faced with the consequences of the recent of the Second Reform Act (1867) in light of the First Reform Act (1832), both of which caused large shifts in the election system in England. The novel takes up many questions and themes, including a surprisingly panoptic and sympathetic study of many different types of characters: even the heroine, Dorothea Brooke, is never beyond Eliot's narrator's reproach, and many good and bad marriages and other social arrangements between the citizens of Middlemarch are tested out through the sprawling narrative. All of Eliot's work is worth read-

https://doi.org/10.1515/9783111561547-013

ing, but *Middlemarch* comes closest to the platonic ideal of a novel, and its challenges force the reader to reconsider and realign their sympathies throughout.

Now on to the novel . . .

Prelude

Who that cares much to know the history of man, and how the mysterious mixture behaves under the varying experiments of Time, has not dwelt, at least briefly, on the life of Saint Theresa, has not smiled with some gentleness at the thought of the little girl walking forth one morning hand-in-hand with her still smaller brother, to go and seek martyrdom in the country of the Moors? Out they toddled from rugged Avila, wide-eyed and helpless-looking as two fawns, but with human hearts, already beating to a national idea; until domestic reality met them in the shape of uncles, and turned them back from their great resolve. That child-pilgrimage was a fit beginning. Theresa's passionate, ideal nature demanded an epic life: what were many-volumed romances of chivalry and the social conquests of a brilliant girl to her? Her flame quickly burned up that light fuel; and, fed from within, soared after some illimitable satisfaction, some object which would never justify weariness, which would reconcile self-despair with the rapturous consciousness of life beyond self. She found her epos in the reform of a religious order.

That Spanish woman who lived three hundred years ago, was certainly not the last of her kind. Many Theresas have been born who found for themselves no epic life wherein there was a constant unfolding of far-resonant action; perhaps only a life of mistakes, the offspring of a certain spiritual grandeur ill-matched with the meanness of opportunity; perhaps a tragic failure which found no sacred poet and sank unwept into oblivion. With dim lights and tangled circumstance they tried to shape their thought and deed in noble agreement; but after all, to common eyes their struggles seemed mere inconsistency and formlessness; for these later-born Theresas were helped by no coherent social faith and order which could perform the function of knowledge for the ardently willing soul. Their ardor alternated between a vague ideal and the common yearning of womanhood; so that the one was disapproved as extravagance, and the other condemned as a lapse.

Some have felt that these blundering lives are due to the inconvenient indefiniteness with which the Supreme Power has fashioned the natures of women: if there were one level of feminine incompetence as strict as the ability to count three and no more, the social lot of women might be treated with scientific certitude. Meanwhile the indefiniteness remains, and the limits of variation are really much wider than any one would imagine from the sameness of women's coiffure and the favorite love-stories in prose and verse. Here and there a cygnet is reared uneasily among the ducklings in the brown pond, and never finds the living stream in fellowship with its own oary-footed kind. Here and there is born a Saint Theresa, foundress of nothing, whose loving heart-beats and sobs after an unattained goodness tremble off and are dispersed among hindrances, instead of centring in some long-recognizable deed.

Chapter XXIX

"I found that no genius in another could please me. My unfortunate paradoxes had entirely dried up that source of comfort." – Goldsmith.

One morning, some weeks after her arrival at Lowick, Dorothea – but why always Dorothea? Was her point of view the only possible one with regard to this marriage? protest against all our interest, all our effort at understanding being given to the young skins that look blooming in spite of trouble; for these too will get faded, and will know the older and more eating griefs which we are helping to neglect. In spite of the blinking eyes and white moles objectionable to Celia, and the want of muscular curve which was morally painful to Sir James, Mr. Casaubon had an intense consciousness within him, and was spiritually a-hungered like the rest of us. He had done nothing exceptional in marrying – nothing but what society sanctions, and considers an occasion for wreaths and bouquets. It had occurred to him that he must not any longer defer his intention of matrimony, and he had reflected that in taking a wife, a man of good position should expect and carefully choose a blooming young lady – the younger the better, because more educable and submissive – of a rank equal to his own, of religious principles, virtuous disposition, and good understanding. On such a young lady he would make handsome settlements, and he would neglect no arrangement for her happiness: in return, he should receive family pleasures and leave behind him that copy of himself which seemed so urgently required of a man – to the sonneteers of the sixteenth century. Times had altered since then, and no sonneteer had insisted on Mr. Casaubon's leaving a copy of himself; moreover, he had not yet succeeded in issuing copies of his mythological key; but he had always intended to acquit himself by marriage, and the sense that he was fast leaving the years behind him, that the world was getting dimmer and that he felt lonely, was a reason to him for losing no more time in overtaking domestic delights before they too were left behind by the years.

And when he had seen Dorothea he believed that he had found even more than he demanded: she might really be such a helpmate to him as would enable him to dispense with a hired secretary, an aid which Mr. Casaubon had never yet employed and had a suspicious dread of. (Mr. Casaubon was nervously conscious that he was expected to manifest a powerful mind.) Providence, in its kindness, had supplied him with the wife he needed. A wife, a modest young lady, with the purely appreciative, unambitious abilities of her sex, is sure to think her husband's mind powerful. Whether Providence had taken equal care of Miss Brooke in presenting her with Mr. Casaubon was an idea which could hardly occur to him. Society never made the preposterous demand that a man should think as much about his own qualifications for making a charming girl happy as he thinks of hers for making himself happy. As if a man could choose not only his wife but his wife's husband! Or as if he were bound to provide charms for his posterity in his own person! – When Dorothea accepted him with effusion, that was only natural; and Mr. Casaubon believed that his happiness was going to begin.

He had not had much foretaste of happiness in his previous life. To know intense joy without a strong bodily frame, one must have an enthusiastic soul. Mr. Casaubon had never had a strong bodily frame, and his soul was sensitive without being enthusiastic: it was too languid to thrill out of self-consciousness into passionate delight; it went on fluttering in the swampy ground where it was hatched, thinking of its wings and never flying. His experience was of that pitiable kind which shrinks from pity, and fears most of all that it should be known: it was that proud narrow sensitiveness which has not mass enough to spare for transformation into sympathy, and quivers thread-like in small currents of self-preoccupation or at best of an egoistic scrupulosity. And Mr. Casaubon had many scruples: he was capable of a severe self-restraint; he was resolute in being a man of honor according to the code; he would be unimpeachable by any recognized opinion. In conduct these ends had been attained; but the difficulty of making his Key to all Mythologies unimpeachable weighed like lead upon his mind; and the pamphlets – or "Parerga" as he called them – by which he tested his public and deposited small monumental records of his march, were far from having been seen in all their significance. He suspected the Archdeacon of not having read them; he was in painful doubt as to what was really thought of them by the leading minds of Brasenose, and bitterly convinced that his old acquaintance Carp had been the writer of that depreciatory recension which was kept locked in a small drawer of Mr. Casaubon's desk, and also in a dark closet of his verbal memory. These were heavy impressions to struggle against, and brought that melancholy embitterment which is the consequence of all excessive claim: even his religious faith wavered with his wavering trust in his own authorship, and the consolations of the Christian hope in immortality seemed to lean on the immortality of the still unwritten Key to all Mythologies. For my part I am very sorry for him. It is an uneasy lot at best, to be what we call highly taught and yet not to enjoy: to be present at this great spectacle of life and never to be liberated from a small hungry shivering self – never to be fully possessed by the glory we behold, never to have our consciousness rapturously transformed into the vividness of a thought, the ardor of a passion, the energy of an action, but always to be scholarly and uninspired, ambitious and timid, scrupulous and dim-sighted. Becoming a dean or even a bishop would make little difference, I fear, to Mr. Casaubon's uneasiness. Doubtless some ancient Greek has observed that behind the big mask and the speaking-trumpet, there must always be our poor little eyes peeping as usual and our timorous lips more or less under anxious control.

To this mental estate mapped out a quarter of a century before, to sensibilities thus fenced in, Mr. Casaubon had thought of annexing happiness with a lovely young bride; but even before marriage, as we have seen, he found himself under a new depression in the consciousness that the new bliss was not blissful to him. Inclination yearned back to its old, easier custom. And the deeper he went in domesticity the more did the sense of acquitting himself and acting with propriety predominate over any other satisfaction. Marriage, like religion and erudition, nay, like authorship itself, was fated to become an outward requirement, and Edward Casaubon was bent on fulfilling unimpeachably all requirements. Even drawing Dorothea into use in his study, according to his own intention before marriage, was an effort which he was always tempted to defer, and but for her pleading insistence it might never have begun. But she had succeeded in making it a matter of course that she should take her place at an early hour in the library and have work either of reading aloud or copying assigned her. The work had been easier to define because Mr. Casaubon had adopted an immediate intention: there was to be a new Parergon, a small monograph on some lately traced indications concerning the Egyptian mysteries whereby certain assertions of Warburton's could be corrected. References were extensive even here, but not altogether shoreless; and sentences were actually to be written in the shape wherein they would be scanned by Brasenose and a less formidable posterity. These minor monumental productions were always exciting to Mr. Casaubon; digestion was made difficult by the interference of citations, or by the rivalry of dialectical phrases ringing against each other in his brain. And from the first there was to be a Latin dedication about which everything was uncertain except that it was not to be addressed to Carp: it was a poisonous regret to Mr. Casaubon that he had once addressed a dedication to Carp in which he had numbered that member of the animal kingdom among the viros nullo aevo perituros, a mistake which would infallibly lay the dedicator open to ridicule in the next age, and might even be chuckled over by Pike and Tench in the present.

Thus Mr. Casaubon was in one of his busiest epochs, and as I began to say a little while ago, Dorothea joined him early in the library where he had breakfasted alone. Celia at this time was on a second visit to Lowick, probably the last before her marriage, and was in the drawing-room expecting Sir James.

Dorothea had learned to read the signs of her husband's mood, and she saw that the morning had become more foggy there during the last hour. She was going silently to her desk when he said, in that distant tone which implied that he was discharging a disagreeable duty –

"Dorothea, here is a letter for you, which was enclosed in one addressed to me."

It was a letter of two pages, and she immediately looked at the signature.

"Mr. Ladislaw! What can he have to say to me?" she exclaimed, in a tone of pleased surprise. "But," she added, looking at Mr. Casaubon, "I can imagine what he has written to you about."

"You can, if you please, read the letter," said Mr. Casaubon, severely pointing to it with his pen, and not looking at her. "But I may as well say beforehand, that I must decline the proposal it contains to pay a visit here. I trust I may be excused for desiring an interval of complete freedom from such distractions as have been hitherto inevitable, and especially from guests whose desultory vivacity makes their presence a fatigue."

There had been no clashing of temper between Dorothea and her husband since that little explosion in Rome, which had left such strong traces in her mind that it had been easier ever since to quell emotion than to incur the consequence of venting it. But this ill-tempered anticipation that she could desire visits which might be disagreeable to her husband, this gratuitous defence of himself against selfish complaint on her part, was too sharp a sting to be meditated on until after it had been resented. Dorothea had thought that she could have been patient with John Milton, but she had never imagined him behaving in this way; and for a moment Mr. Casaubon seemed to be stupidly undiscerning and odiously unjust. Pity, that "new-born babe" which was by-and-by to rule many a storm within her, did not "stride the blast" on this occasion. With her first words, uttered in a tone that shook him, she startled Mr. Casaubon into looking at her, and meeting the flash of her eyes.

"Why do you attribute to me a wish for anything that would annoy you? You speak to me as if I were something you had to contend against. Wait at least till I appear to consult my own pleasure apart from yours."

"Dorothea, you are hasty," answered Mr. Casaubon, nervously.

Decidedly, this woman was too young to be on the formidable level of wife-hood – unless she had been pale and feature less and taken everything for granted.

"I think it was you who were first hasty in your false suppositions about my feeling," said Dorothea, in the same tone. The fire was not dissipated yet, and she thought it was ignoble in her husband not to apologize to her.

"We will, if you please, say no more on this subject, Dorothea. I have neither leisure nor energy for this kind of debate."

Here Mr. Casaubon dipped his pen and made as if he would return to his writing, though his hand trembled so much that the words seemed to be written in an unknown character. There are answers which, in turning away wrath, only send it to the other end of the room, and to have a discussion coolly waived when you feel that justice is all on your own side is even more exasperating in marriage than in philosophy.

Dorothea left Ladislaw's two letters unread on her husband's writing-table and went to her own place, the scorn and indignation within her rejecting the reading of these letters, just as we hurl away any trash towards which we seem to have been suspected of mean cupidity. She did not in the least divine the subtle sources of her husband's bad temper about these letters: she only knew that they had caused him to offend her. She began to work at once, and her hand did not tremble; on the contrary, in writing out the quotations which had been given to her the day before, she felt that she was forming her letters beautifully, and it seemed to her that she saw the construction of the Latin she was copying, and which she was beginning to understand, more clearly than usual. In her indignation there was a sense of superiority, but it went out for the present in firmness of stroke, and did not compress itself into an inward articulate voice pronouncing the once "affable archangel" a poor creature.

There had been this apparent quiet for half an hour, and Dorothea had not looked away from her own table, when she heard the loud bang of a book on the floor, and turning quickly saw Mr. Casaubon on the library steps clinging forward as if he were in some bodily distress. She started up and bounded towards him in an instant: he was evidently in great straits for breath. Jumping on a stool she got close to his elbow and said with her whole soul melted into tender alarm –

"Can you lean on me, dear?"

He was still for two or three minutes, which seemed endless to her, unable to speak or move, gasping for breath. When at last he descended the three steps and fell backward in the large chair which Dorothea had drawn close to the foot of the ladder, he no longer gasped but seemed helpless and about to faint. Dorothea rang the bell violently, and presently Mr. Casaubon was helped to the couch: he did not faint, and was gradually reviving, when Sir James Chettam came in, having been met in the hall with the news that Mr. Casaubon had "had a fit in the library."

"Good God! this is just what might have been expected," was his immediate thought. If his prophetic soul had been urged to particularize, it seemed to him that "fits" would have been the definite expression alighted upon. He asked his informant, the butler, whether the doctor had been sent for. The butler never knew his master want the doctor before; but would it not be right to send for a physician?

When Sir James entered the library, however, Mr. Casaubon could make some signs of his usual politeness, and Dorothea, who in the reaction from her first terror had been kneeling and sobbing by his side now rose and herself proposed that some one should ride off for a medical man.

"I recommend you to send for Lydgate," said Sir James. "My mother has called him in, and she has found him uncommonly clever. She has had a poor opinion of the physicians since my father's death."

Dorothea appealed to her husband, and he made a silent sign of approval. So Mr. Lydgate was sent for and he came wonderfully soon, for the messenger, who was Sir James Chettam's man and knew Mr. Lydgate, met him leading his horse along the Lowick road and giving his arm to Miss Vincy.

Celia, in the drawing-room, had known nothing of the trouble till Sir James told her of it. After Dorothea's account, he no longer considered the illness a fit, but still something "of that nature."

"Poor dear Dodo – how dreadful!" said Celia, feeling as much grieved as her own perfect happiness would allow. Her little hands were clasped, and enclosed by Sir James's as a bud is enfolded by a liberal calyx. "It is very shocking that Mr. Casaubon should be ill; but I never did like him. And I think he is not half fond enough of Dorothea; and he ought to be, for I am sure no one else would have had him – do you think they would?"

"I always thought it a horrible sacrifice of your sister," said Sir James.

"Yes. But poor Dodo never did do what other people do, and I think she never will."

"She is a noble creature," said the loyal-hearted Sir James. He had just had a fresh impression of this kind, as he had seen Dorothea stretching her tender arm under her husband's neck and looking at him with unspeakable sorrow. He did not know how much penitence there was in the sorrow.

"Yes," said Celia, thinking it was very well for Sir James to say so, but HE would not have been comfortable with Dodo. "Shall I go to her? Could I help her, do you think?"

"I think it would be well for you just to go and see her before Lydgate comes," said Sir James, magnanimously. "Only don't stay long."

While Celia was gone he walked up and down remembering what he had originally felt about Dorothea's engagement, and feeling a revival of his disgust at Mr. Brooke's indifference. If Cadwallader – if every one else had regarded the affair as he, Sir James, had done, the marriage might have been hindered. It was wicked to let a young girl blindly decide her fate in that way, without any effort to save her. Sir James had long ceased to have any regrets on his own account:

his heart was satisfied with his engagement to Celia. But he had a chivalrous nature (was not the disinterested service of woman among the ideal glories of old chivalry?): his disregarded love had not turned to bitterness; its death had made sweet odors – floating memories that clung with a consecrating effect to Dorothea. He could remain her brotherly friend, interpreting her actions with generous trustfulness.

Oscar Wilde's *The Picture of Dorian Gray*

Printed in 1890 in London. Available on Project Gutenberg, https://www.gutenberg.org/ebooks/174/ [last access 27.11.2024].

Image 13: Aubrey Beardsley, "The Climax," 1893.

About *The Picture of Dorian Gray*
Part philosophical treatise on art, part Gothic novel, part sumptuous thriller, *The Picture of Dorian Gray* (1890) is Oscar Wilde's only novel. Wilde was born in 1854 and died in 1900, and was during

https://doi.org/10.1515/9783111561547-014

his life a figure of great intrigue in London and beyond. He was convicted for "gross indecency" for his homosexuality and jailed from 1895 to 1897, and had been only a few years prior one of the most beloved playwrights of the century. Included here is an excerpt from the preface to the novel, as Wilde tests differing ideals of art and the artist that will later be at play in the text: the painter Basil Hallward will, early in the novel, paint the titular picture that will bear Dorian Gray's age and sins in his stead. His supernatural youth and beauty lead to increasingly shocking scenes, including murders, suicides, squalor, and decadent opulence. As Dorian's soul grows increasingly corrupted by his actions, the painting, looming so large even in the outset of the novel, becomes his absolute fixation. Meditating on art, Wilde's novel is perhaps best read as a contemplation of the role of art and artists in society, and its beautiful, rich prose is snug and content, punctured by sudden bursts of violence and action.

Now on to the novel . . .

The Preface

The artist is the creator of beautiful things. To reveal art and conceal the artist is art's aim. The critic is he who can translate into another manner or a new material his impression of beautiful things.

The highest as the lowest form of criticism is a mode of autobiography. Those who find ugly meanings in beautiful things are corrupt without being charming. This is a fault.

Those who find beautiful meanings in beautiful things are the cultivated. For these there is hope. They are the elect to whom beautiful things mean only beauty.

There is no such thing as a moral or an immoral book. Books are well written, or badly written. That is all.

The nineteenth century dislike of realism is the rage of Caliban seeing his own face in a glass.

The nineteenth century dislike of romanticism is the rage of Caliban not seeing his own face in a glass. The moral life of man forms part of the subject-matter of the artist, but the morality of art consists in the perfect use of an imperfect medium. No artist desires to prove anything. Even things that are true can be proved. No artist has ethical sympathies. An ethical sympathy in an artist is an unpardonable mannerism of style. No artist is ever morbid. The artist can express everything. Thought and language are to the artist instruments of an art. Vice and virtue are to the artist materials for an art. From the point of view of form, the type of all the arts is the art of the musician. From the point of view of feeling, the actor's craft is the type. All art is at once surface and symbol. Those who go beneath the surface do so at their peril. Those who read the symbol do so at their peril. It is the spectator, and not life, that art really mirrors. Diversity of opinion about a work of art shows that the work is new, complex, and vital. When critics disagree, the artist is in accord with himself. We can forgive a man for making a useful thing as long as he does not admire it. The only excuse for making a useless thing is that one admires it intensely.

All art is quite useless.

Chapter I

The studio was filled with the rich odour of roses, and when the light summer wind stirred amidst the trees of the garden, there came through the open door the heavy scent of the lilac, or the more delicate perfume of the pink-flowering thorn.

From the corner of the divan of Persian saddle-bags on which he was lying, smoking, as was his custom, innumerable cigarettes, Lord Henry Wotton could just catch the gleam of the honey-sweet and honey-coloured blossoms of a laburnum, whose tremulous branches seemed hardly able to bear the burden of a beauty so flamelike as theirs; and now and then the fantastic shadows of birds in flight flitted across the long tussore-silk curtains that were stretched in front of the huge window, producing a kind of momentary Japanese effect, and making him think of those pallid, jade-faced painters of Tokyo who, through the medium of an art that is necessarily immobile, seek to convey the sense of swiftness and motion. The sullen murmur of the bees shouldering their way through the long unmown grass, or circling with monotonous insistence round the dusty gilt horns of the straggling woodbine, seemed to make the stillness more oppressive. The dim roar of London was like the bourdon note of a distant organ.

In the centre of the room, clamped to an upright easel, stood the full-length portrait of a young man of extraordinary personal beauty, and in front of it, some little distance away, was sitting the artist himself, Basil Hallward, whose sudden disappearance some years ago caused, at the time, such public excitement and gave rise to so many strange conjectures.

As the painter looked at the gracious and comely form he had so skilfully mirrored in his art, a smile of pleasure passed across his face, and seemed about to linger there. But he suddenly started up, and closing his eyes, placed his fingers upon the lids, as though he sought to imprison within his brain some curious dream from which he feared he might awake.

"It is your best work, Basil, the best thing you have ever done," said Lord Henry languidly. "You must certainly send it next year to the Grosvenor. The Academy is too large and too vulgar. Whenever I have gone there, there have been either so many people that I have not been able to see the pictures, which was dreadful, or so many pictures that I have not been able to see the people, which was worse. The Grosvenor is really the only place."

"I don't think I shall send it anywhere," he answered, tossing his head back in that odd way that used to make his friends laugh at him at Oxford. "No, I won't send it anywhere."

Lord Henry elevated his eyebrows and looked at him in amazement through the thin blue wreaths of smoke that curled up in such fanciful whorls from his heavy, opium-tainted cigarette. "Not send it anywhere? My dear fellow, why? Have you any reason? What odd chaps you painters are! You do anything in the world to gain a reputation. As soon as you have one, you seem to want to throw it away. It is silly of you, for there is only one thing in the world worse than being talked about, and that is not being talked about. A portrait like this would set you far above all the young men in England, and make the old men quite jealous, if old men are ever capable of any emotion."

"I know you will laugh at me," he replied, "but I really can't exhibit it. I have put too much of myself into it."

Lord Henry stretched himself out on the divan and laughed.

"Yes, I knew you would; but it is quite true, all the same."

"Too much of yourself in it! Upon my word, Basil, I didn't know you were so vain; and I really can't see any resemblance between you, with your rugged strong face and your coal-black hair, and this young Adonis, who looks as if he was made out of ivory and rose-leaves. Why, my dear Basil, he is a Narcissus, and you – well, of course you have an intellectual expression and all that. But beauty, real beauty, ends where an intellectual expression begins. Intellect is in itself a mode of exaggeration, and destroys the harmony of any face. The moment one sits down to think, one becomes all nose, or all forehead, or something horrid. Look at the successful men in any of the learned professions. How perfectly hideous they are! Except, of course, in the Church. But then in the Church they don't think. A bishop keeps on saying at the age of eighty what he was told to say when he was a boy of eighteen, and as a natural consequence he always looks absolutely delightful. Your mysterious young friend, whose name you have never told me, but whose picture really fascinates me, never thinks. I feel quite sure of that. He is some brainless beautiful creature who should be always here in winter when we have no flowers to look at, and always here in summer when we want something to chill our intelligence. Don't flatter yourself, Basil: you are not in the least like him."

"You don't understand me, Harry," answered the artist. "Of course I am not like him. I know that perfectly well. Indeed, I should be sorry to look like him. You shrug your shoulders? I am telling you the truth. There is a fatality about all physical and intellectual distinction, the sort of fatality that seems to dog through history the faltering steps of kings. It is better not to be different from one's fellows. The ugly and the stupid have the best of it in this world. They can sit at their ease and gape at the play. If they know nothing of victory, they are at least spared the knowledge of defeat. They live as we all should live – undisturbed, indifferent, and without disquiet. They neither bring ruin upon others, nor ever receive it from alien hands. Your rank and wealth, Harry; my brains, such as they are – my art, whatever it may be worth; Dorian Gray's good looks – we shall all suffer for what the gods have given us, suffer terribly."

"Dorian Gray? Is that his name?" asked Lord Henry, walking across the studio towards Basil Hallward.

"Yes, that is his name. I didn't intend to tell it to you."

"But why not?"

"Oh, I can't explain. When I like people immensely, I never tell their names to any one. It is like surrendering a part of them. I have grown to love secrecy. It seems to be the one thing that can make modern life mysterious or marvellous to us. The commonest thing is delightful if one only hides it. When I leave town now I never tell my people where I am going. If I did, I would lose all my pleasure. It is a silly habit, I dare say, but somehow it seems to bring a great deal of romance into one's life. I suppose you think me awfully foolish about it?"

"Not at all," answered Lord Henry, "not at all, my dear Basil. You seem to forget that I am married, and the one charm of marriage is that it makes a life of deception absolutely necessary for both parties. I never know where my wife is, and my wife never knows what I am doing. When we meet – we do meet occasionally, when we dine out together, or go down to the Duke's – we tell each other the most absurd stories with the most serious faces. My wife is very good at it – much better, in fact, than I am. She never gets confused over her dates, and I always do. But when she does find me out, she makes no row at all. I sometimes wish she would; but she merely laughs at me."

"I hate the way you talk about your married life, Harry," said Basil Hallward, strolling towards the door that led into the garden. "I believe that you are really a very good husband, but that you are thoroughly ashamed of your own virtues. You are an extraordinary fellow. You never say a moral thing, and you never do a wrong thing. Your cynicism is simply a pose."

"Being natural is simply a pose, and the most irritating pose I know," cried Lord Henry, laughing; and the two young men went out into the garden together and ensconced themselves on a long bamboo seat that stood in the shade of a tall laurel bush. The sunlight slipped over the polished leaves. In the grass, white daisies were tremulous.

After a pause, Lord Henry pulled out his watch. "I am afraid I must be going, Basil," he murmured, "and before I go, I insist on your answering a question I put to you some time ago."

"What is that?" said the painter, keeping his eyes fixed on the ground.

"You know quite well."

"I do not, Harry."

"Well, I will tell you what it is. I want you to explain to me why you won't exhibit Dorian Gray's picture. I want the real reason."

"I told you the real reason."

"No, you did not. You said it was because there was too much of yourself in it. Now, that is childish."

"Harry," said Basil Hallward, looking him straight in the face, "every portrait that is painted with feeling is a portrait of the artist, not of the sitter. The sitter is merely the accident, the occasion. It is not he who is revealed by the painter; it is rather the painter who, on the coloured canvas, reveals himself. The reason I will not exhibit this picture is that I am afraid that I have shown in it the secret of my own soul."

Lord Henry laughed. "And what is that?" he asked.

"I will tell you," said Hallward; but an expression of perplexity came over his face.

"I am all expectation, Basil," continued his companion, glancing at him.

"Oh, there is really very little to tell, Harry," answered the painter; "and I am afraid you will hardly understand it. Perhaps you will hardly believe it."

Lord Henry smiled, and leaning down, plucked a pink-petalled daisy from the grass and examined it. "I am quite sure I shall understand it," he replied, gazing intently at the little golden, white-feathered disk, "and as for believing things, I can believe anything, provided that it is quite incredible."

The wind shook some blossoms from the trees, and the heavy lilac-blooms, with their clustering stars, moved to and fro in the languid air. A grasshopper began to chirrup by the wall, and like a blue thread a long thin dragon-fly floated past on its brown gauze wings. Lord Henry felt as if he could hear Basil Hallward's heart beating, and wondered what was coming.

"The story is simply this," said the painter after some time. "Two months ago I went to a crush at Lady Brandon's. You know we poor artists have to show ourselves in society from time to time, just to remind the public that we are not savages. With an evening coat and a white tie, as you told me once, anybody, even a stock-broker, can gain a reputation for being civilized. Well, after I had been in the room about ten minutes, talking to huge overdressed dowagers and tedious academicians, I suddenly became conscious that some one was looking at me. I turned half-way round and saw Dorian Gray for the first time. When our eyes met, I felt that I was growing pale. A curious sensation of terror came over me. I knew that I had come face to face with some one whose mere personality was so fascinating that, if I allowed it to do so, it would absorb my whole nature, my whole soul, my very art itself. I did not want any external influence in my life. You know yourself, Harry, how independent I am by nature. I have always been my own master; had at least always been so, till I met Dorian Gray. Then – but I don't know how to explain it to you. Something seemed to tell me that I was on the verge of a terrible crisis in my life. I had a strange feeling that fate had in store for me exquisite joys and exquisite sorrows. I grew afraid and turned to quit the room. It was not conscience that made me do so: it was a sort of cowardice. I take no credit to myself for trying to escape."

"Conscience and cowardice are really the same things, Basil. Conscience is the trade-name of the firm. That is all."

"I don't believe that, Harry, and I don't believe you do either. However, whatever was my motive – and it may have been pride, for I used to be very proud – I certainly struggled to the door. There, of course, I stumbled against Lady Brandon. 'You are not going to run away so soon, Mr. Hallward?' she screamed out. You know her curiously shrill voice?"

"Yes; she is a peacock in everything but beauty," said Lord Henry, pulling the daisy to bits with his long nervous fingers.

"I could not get rid of her. She brought me up to royalties, and people with stars and garters, and elderly ladies with gigantic tiaras and parrot noses. She spoke of me as her dearest friend. I had only met her once before, but she took it into her head to lionize me. I believe some picture of mine had made a great success at the time, at least had been chattered about in the penny newspapers, which is the nineteenth-century standard of immortality. Suddenly I found myself face to face with the young man whose personality had so strangely stirred me. We were quite close, almost touching. Our eyes met again. It was reckless of me, but I asked Lady Brandon to introduce me to him. Perhaps it was not so reckless, after all. It was simply inevitable. We would have spoken to each other without any introduction. I am sure of that. Dorian told me so afterwards. He, too, felt that we were destined to know each other."

"And how did Lady Brandon describe this wonderful young man?" asked his companion. "I know she goes in for giving a rapid precis of all her guests. I remember her bringing me up to a truculent and red-faced old gentleman covered all over with orders and ribbons, and hissing into my ear, in a tragic whisper which must have been perfectly audible to everybody in the room, the most astounding details. I simply fled. I like to find out people for myself. But Lady Brandon treats her guests exactly as an auctioneer treats his goods. She either explains them entirely away, or tells one everything about them except what one wants to know."

"Poor Lady Brandon! You are hard on her, Harry!" said Hallward listlessly.

"My dear fellow, she tried to found a salon, and only succeeded in opening a restaurant. How could I admire her? But tell me, what did she say about Mr. Dorian Gray?"

"Oh, something like, 'Charming boy – poor dear mother and I absolutely inseparable. Quite forget what he does – afraid he – doesn't do anything – oh, yes, plays the piano – or is it the violin, dear Mr. Gray?' Neither of us could help laughing, and we became friends at once."

"Laughter is not at all a bad beginning for a friendship, and it is far the best ending for one," said the young lord, plucking another daisy.

Hallward shook his head. "You don't understand what friendship is, Harry," he murmured – "or what enmity is, for that matter. You like every one; that is to say, you are indifferent to every one."

"How horribly unjust of you!" cried Lord Henry, tilting his hat back and looking up at the little clouds that, like ravelled skeins of glossy white silk, were drifting across the hollowed turquoise of the summer sky. "Yes; horribly unjust of you. I make a great difference between people. I choose my friends for their good looks, my acquaintances for their good characters, and my enemies for their good intellects. A man cannot be too careful in the choice of his enemies. I have not got one who is a fool. They are all men of some intellectual power, and consequently they all appreciate me. Is that very vain of me? I think it is rather vain."

"I should think it was, Harry. But according to your category I must be merely an acquaintance."

"My dear old Basil, you are much more than an acquaintance."

"And much less than a friend. A sort of brother, I suppose?"

"Oh, brothers! I don't care for brothers. My elder brother won't die, and my younger brothers seem never to do anything else."

"Harry!" exclaimed Hallward, frowning.

"My dear fellow, I am not quite serious. But I can't help detesting my relations. I suppose it comes from the fact that none of us can stand other people having the same faults as ourselves. I quite sympathize with the rage of the English democracy against what they call the vices of the upper orders. The masses feel that drunkenness, stupidity, and immorality should be their own special property, and that if any one of us makes an ass of himself, he is poaching on their preserves. When poor Southwark got into the divorce court, their indignation was quite magnificent. And yet I don't suppose that ten per cent of the proletariat live correctly."

"I don't agree with a single word that you have said, and, what is more, Harry, I feel sure you don't either."

Lord Henry stroked his pointed brown beard and tapped the toe of his patent-leather boot with a tasselled ebony cane. "How English you are Basil! That is the second time you have made that observation. If one puts forward an idea to a true Englishman – always a rash thing to do – he never dreams of considering whether the idea is right or wrong. The only thing he considers of any importance is whether one believes it oneself. Now, the value of an idea has nothing whatsoever to do with the sincerity of the man who expresses it. Indeed, the probabilities are that the more insincere the man is, the more purely intellectual will the idea be, as in that case it will not be coloured by either his wants, his desires, or his prejudices. However, I don't propose to discuss politics, sociology, or metaphysics with you. I like persons better than principles, and I like persons with no principles better than anything else in the world. Tell me more about Mr. Dorian Gray. How often do you see him?"

"Every day. I couldn't be happy if I didn't see him every day. He is absolutely necessary to me."

"How extraordinary! I thought you would never care for anything but your art."

"He is all my art to me now," said the painter gravely. "I sometimes think, Harry, that there are only two eras of any importance in the world's history. The first is the appearance of a new medium for art, and the second is the appearance of a new personality for art also. What the invention of oil-painting was to the Venetians, the face of Antinous was to late Greek sculpture, and the face of Dorian Gray will some day be to me. It is not merely that I paint from him, draw from him, sketch from him. Of course, I have done all that. But he is much more to me than a model or a sitter. I won't tell you that I am dissatisfied with what I have done of him, or that his beauty is such that art cannot express it. There is nothing that art cannot express, and I know that the work I have done, since I met Dorian Gray, is good work, is the best work of my life. But in some curious way – I wonder will you understand me? – his personality has suggested to me an entirely new manner in art, an entirely new mode of style. I see things differently, I think of them differently. I can now recreate life in a way that was hidden from me before. 'A dream of form in days of thought' – who is it who says that? I forget; but it is what Dorian Gray has been to me. The merely visible presence of this lad – for he seems to me little more than a lad, though he is really over twenty – his merely visible presence – ah! I wonder can you realize all that that means? Unconsciously he defines for me the lines of a fresh school, a school that is to have in it all the passion of the romantic spirit, all the perfection of the spirit that is Greek. The harmony of soul and body – how much that is! We in our madness have separated the two, and have invented a realism that is vulgar, an ideality that is void. Harry! if you only knew what Dorian Gray is to me! You remember that landscape of mine, for which Agnew offered me such a huge price but which I would not part with? It is one of the best things I have ever done. And why is it so? Because, while I was painting it, Dorian Gray sat beside me. Some subtle influence passed from him to me, and for the first time in my life I saw in the plain woodland the wonder I had always looked for and always missed."

"Basil, this is extraordinary! I must see Dorian Gray."

Hallward got up from the seat and walked up and down the garden. After some time he came back. "Harry," he said, "Dorian Gray is to me simply a motive in art. You might see nothing in him. I see everything in him. He is never more present in my work than when no image of him is there. He is a suggestion, as I have said, of a new manner. I find him in the curves of certain lines, in the loveliness and subtleties of certain colours. That is all."

"Then why won't you exhibit his portrait?" asked Lord Henry.

"Because, without intending it, I have put into it some expression of all this curious artistic idolatry, of which, of course, I have never cared to speak to him. He knows nothing about it. He shall never know anything about it. But the world might guess it, and I will not bare my soul to their shallow prying eyes. My heart shall never be put under their microscope. There is too much of myself in the thing, Harry – too much of myself!"

"Poets are not so scrupulous as you are. They know how useful passion is for publication. Nowadays a broken heart will run to many editions."

"I hate them for it," cried Hallward. "An artist should create beautiful things, but should put nothing of his own life into them. We live in an age when men treat art as if it were meant to be a form of autobiography. We have lost the abstract sense of beauty. Some day I will show the world what it is; and for that reason the world shall never see my portrait of Dorian Gray."

"I think you are wrong, Basil, but I won't argue with you. It is only the intellectually lost who ever argue. Tell me, is Dorian Gray very fond of you?"

The painter considered for a few moments. "He likes me," he answered after a pause; "I know he likes me. Of course I flatter him dreadfully. I find a strange pleasure in saying things to him that I know I shall be sorry for having said. As a rule, he is charming to me, and we sit in the studio and talk of a thousand things. Now and then, however, he is horribly thoughtless, and seems to take a real delight in giving me pain. Then I feel, Harry, that I have given away my whole soul to some one who treats it as if it were a flower to put in his coat, a bit of decoration to charm his vanity, an ornament for a summer's day."

"Days in summer, Basil, are apt to linger," murmured Lord Henry. "Perhaps you will tire sooner than he will. It is a sad thing to think of, but there is no doubt that genius lasts longer than beauty. That accounts for the fact that we all take such pains to over-educate ourselves. In the wild struggle for existence, we want to have something that endures, and so we fill our minds with rubbish and facts, in the silly hope of keeping our place. The thoroughly well-informed man – that is the modern ideal. And the mind of the thoroughly well-informed man is a dreadful thing. It is like a bric-a-brac shop, all monsters and dust, with everything priced above its proper value. I think you will tire first, all the same. Some day you will look at your friend, and he will seem to you to be a little out of drawing, or you won't like his tone of colour, or something. You will bitterly reproach him in your own heart, and seriously think that he has behaved very badly to you. The next time he calls, you will be perfectly cold and indifferent. It will be a great pity, for it will alter you. What you have told me is quite a romance, a romance of art one might call it, and the worst of having a romance of any kind is that it leaves one so unromantic."

"Harry, don't talk like that. As long as I live, the personality of Dorian Gray will dominate me. You can't feel what I feel. You change too often."

"Ah, my dear Basil, that is exactly why I can feel it. Those who are faithful know only the trivial side of love: it is the faithless who know love's tragedies." And Lord Henry struck a light on a dainty silver case and began to smoke a cigarette with a self-conscious and satisfied air, as if he had summed up the world in a phrase. There was a rustle of chirruping sparrows in the green lacquer leaves of the ivy, and the blue cloud-shadows chased themselves across the grass like swallows. How pleasant it was in the garden! And how delightful other people's emotions were! – much more delightful than their ideas, it seemed to him. One's own soul, and the passions of one's friends – those were the fascinating things in life. He pictured to himself with silent amusement the tedious luncheon that he had missed by staying so long with Basil Hallward. Had he gone to his aunt's, he would have been sure to have met Lord Goodbody there, and the whole conversation would have been about the feeding of the poor and the necessity for model lodging-houses. Each class would have preached the importance of those virtues, for whose exercise there was no necessity in their own lives. The rich would have spoken on the value of thrift, and the idle grown eloquent over the dignity of labour. It was charming to have escaped all that! As he thought of his aunt, an idea seemed to strike him. He turned to Hallward and said, "My dear fellow, I have just remembered."

"Remembered what, Harry?"

"Where I heard the name of Dorian Gray."

"Where was it?" asked Hallward, with a slight frown.

"Don't look so angry, Basil. It was at my aunt, Lady Agatha's. She told me she had discovered a wonderful young man who was going to help her in the East

End, and that his name was Dorian Gray. I am bound to state that she never told me he was good-looking. Women have no appreciation of good looks; at least, good women have not. She said that he was very earnest and had a beautiful nature. I at once pictured to myself a creature with spectacles and lank hair, horribly freckled, and tramping about on huge feet. I wish I had known it was your friend."

"I am very glad you didn't, Harry."

"Why?"

"I don't want you to meet him."

"You don't want me to meet him?"

"No."

"Mr. Dorian Gray is in the studio, sir," said the butler, coming into the garden.

"You must introduce me now," cried Lord Henry, laughing.

The painter turned to his servant, who stood blinking in the sunlight. "Ask Mr. Gray to wait, Parker: I shall be in in a few moments." The man bowed and went up the walk.

Then he looked at Lord Henry. "Dorian Gray is my dearest friend," he said. "He has a simple and a beautiful nature. Your aunt was quite right in what she said of him. Don't spoil him. Don't try to influence him. Your influence would be bad. The world is wide, and has many marvellous people in it. Don't take away from me the one person who gives to my art whatever charm it possesses: my life as an artist depends on him. Mind, Harry, I trust you." He spoke very slowly, and the words seemed wrung out of him almost against his will.

"What nonsense you talk!" said Lord Henry, smiling, and taking Hallward by the arm, he almost led him into the house.

H.G. Wells' *The Time Machine*

Printed in 1895 in London. Available on Project Gutenberg at https://www.gutenberg.org/ebooks/35/ [last access 27.11.2024].

Image 14: James Abbott McNeill Whistler, "Nocturne in Black and Gold, the Falling Rocket," 1875.

About *The Time Machine*
H.G. Wells (1866–1946) wrote some fifty novels and many more pieces of short fiction, including in his science fiction and speculative fiction much social commentary, satire, and many political theories. *The Time Machine*, first published in 1895 and never out of print, is one of his many superb and gripping tales, but an interested reader might also recognize many of his other titles,

including *The Invisible Man*, *The Island of Doctor Moreau*, and *The War of the Worlds*. *The Time Machine* takes up many of the themes Wells would write on throughout his career, including a sharp piece of social commentary in the Eloi, childlike, pure creatures in the far future, and the monstrous Morlocks, underground predators of the Eloi: the former are the distant descendants of the wealthy, and the latter the poor. Wells' time traveler, a gentleman scientist, encounters these and many other compelling and frightening remnants of humanity millions and billions of years into the future. Writing in the late-century, Wells represents a turning point as the Victorians started to consider what might come after their era had ended, and what the future of the society they took so much pride in might look like.

Now on to the Novel . . .

Chapter IV

Time Travelling

'I told some of you last Thursday of the principles of the Time Machine, and showed you the actual thing itself, incomplete in the workshop. There it is now, a little travel-worn, truly; and one of the ivory bars is cracked, and a brass rail bent; but the rest of it's sound enough. I expected to finish it on Friday, but on Friday, when the putting together was nearly done, I found that one of the nickel bars was exactly one inch too short, and this I had to get remade; so that the thing was not complete until this morning. It was at ten o'clock to-day that the first of all Time Machines began its career. I gave it a last tap, tried all the screws again, put one more drop of oil on the quartz rod, and sat myself in the saddle. I suppose a suicide who holds a pistol to his skull feels much the same wonder at what will come next as I felt then. I took the starting lever in one hand and the stopping one in the other, pressed the first, and almost immediately the second. I seemed to reel; I felt a nightmare sensation of falling; and, looking round, I saw the laboratory exactly as before. Had anything happened? For a moment I suspected that my intellect had tricked me. Then I noted the clock. A moment before, as it seemed, it had stood at a minute or so past ten; now it was nearly half-past three!

'I drew a breath, set my teeth, gripped the starting lever with both hands, and went off with a thud. The laboratory got hazy and went dark. Mrs. Watchett came in and walked, apparently without seeing me, towards the garden door. I suppose it took her a minute or so to traverse the place, but to me she seemed to shoot across the room like a rocket. I pressed the lever over to its extreme position. The night came like the turning out of a lamp, and in another moment came to-morrow. The laboratory grew faint and hazy, then fainter and ever fainter. To-morrow night came black, then day again, night again, day again, faster and faster still. An eddying murmur filled my ears, and a strange, dumb confusedness descended on my mind.

'I am afraid I cannot convey the peculiar sensations of time travelling. They are excessively unpleasant. There is a feeling exactly like that one has upon a switchback – of a helpless headlong motion! I felt the same horrible anticipation, too, of an imminent smash. As I put on pace, night followed day like the flapping of a black wing. The dim suggestion of the laboratory seemed presently to fall away from me, and I saw the sun hopping swiftly across the sky, leaping it every minute, and every minute marking a day. I supposed the laboratory had been destroyed and I had come into the open air. I had a dim impression of scaffolding, but I was already going too fast to be conscious of any moving things. The slowest snail that ever crawled dashed by too fast for me. The twinkling succession of darkness and light was excessively painful to the eye. Then, in the intermittent darknesses, I saw the moon spinning swiftly through her quarters from new to full, and had a faint glimpse of the circling stars. Presently, as I went on, still gaining velocity, the palpitation of night and day merged into one continuous greyness; the sky took on a wonderful deepness of blue, a splendid luminous color like that of early twilight; the jerking sun became a streak of fire, a brilliant arch, in space; the moon a fainter fluctuating band; and I could see nothing of the stars, save now and then a brighter circle flickering in the blue.

'The landscape was misty and vague. I was still on the hill-side upon which this house now stands, and the shoulder rose above me grey and dim. I saw trees growing and changing like puffs of vapour, now brown, now green; they grew, spread, shivered, and passed away. I saw huge buildings rise up faint and fair, and pass like dreams. The whole surface of the earth seemed changed – melting and flowing under my eyes. The little hands upon the dials that registered my speed raced round faster and faster. Presently I noted that the sun belt swayed up and down, from solstice to solstice, in a minute or less, and that consequently my pace was over a year a minute; and minute by minute the white snow flashed across the world, and vanished, and was followed by the bright, brief green of spring.

'The unpleasant sensations of the start were less poignant now. They merged at last into a kind of hysterical exhilaration. I remarked indeed a clumsy swaying of the machine, for which I was unable to account. But my mind was too confused to attend to it, so with a kind of madness growing upon me, I flung myself into futurity. At first I scarce thought of stopping, scarce thought of anything but these new sensations. But presently a fresh series of impressions grew up in my mind – a certain curiosity and therewith a certain dread – until at last they took complete possession of me. What strange developments of humanity, what wonderful advances upon our rudimentary civilization, I thought, might not appear when I came to look nearly into the dim elusive world that raced and fluctuated before my eyes! I saw great and splendid architecture rising about me, more massive than any buildings of our own time, and yet, as it seemed, built of glimmer and mist. I saw a richer green flow up the hill-side, and remain there, without any wintry intermission. Even through the veil of my confusion the earth seemed very fair. And so my mind came round to the business of stopping,

'The peculiar risk lay in the possibility of my finding some substance in the space which I, or the machine, occupied. So long as I travelled at a high velocity through time, this scarcely mattered; I was, so to speak, attenuated – was slipping like a vapour through the interstices of intervening substances! But to come to a stop involved the jamming of myself, molecule by molecule, into whatever lay in my way; meant bringing my atoms into such intimate contact with those of the obstacle that a profound chemical reaction – possibly a far-reaching explosion – would result, and blow myself and my apparatus out of all possible dimensions – into the Unknown. This possibility had occurred to me again and again while I was making the machine; but then I had cheerfully accepted it as an unavoidable risk – one of the risks a man has got to take! Now the risk was inevitable, I no longer saw it in the same cheerful light. The fact is that insensibly, the absolute strangeness of everything, the sickly jarring and swaying of the machine, above all, the feeling of prolonged falling, had absolutely upset my nerve. I told myself that I could never stop, and with a gust of petulance I resolved to stop forthwith. Like an impatient fool, I lugged over the lever, and incontinently the thing went reeling over, and I was flung headlong through the air.

'There was the sound of a clap of thunder in my ears. I may have been stunned for a moment. A pitiless hail was hissing round me, and I was sitting on soft turf in front of the overset machine. Everything still seemed grey, but presently I remarked that the confusion in my ears was gone. I looked round me. I was on what seemed to be a little lawn in a garden, surrounded by rhododendron bushes, and I noticed that their mauve and purple blossoms were dropping in a shower under the beating of the hail-stones. The rebounding, dancing hail hung in a cloud over the machine, and drove along the ground like smoke. In a moment I was wet to the skin. "Fine hospitality," said I, "to a man who has travelled innumerable years to see you."

'Presently I thought what a fool I was to get wet. I stood up and looked round me. A colossal figure, carved apparently in some white stone, loomed indistinctly beyond the rhododendrons through the hazy downpour. But all else of the world was invisible.

'My sensations would be hard to describe. As the columns of hail grew thinner, I saw the white figure more distinctly. It was very large, for a silver birch-tree touched its shoulder. It was of white marble, in shape something like a winged sphinx, but the wings, instead of being carried vertically at the sides, were spread so that it seemed to hover. The pedestal, it appeared to me, was of bronze, and was thick with verdigris. It chanced that the face was towards me; the sightless eyes seemed to watch me; there was the faint shadow of a smile on the lips. It was greatly weather-worn, and that imparted an unpleasant suggestion of disease. I stood looking at it for a little space – half a minute, perhaps, or half an hour. It seemed to advance and to recede as the hail drove before it denser or thinner. At last I tore my eyes from it for a moment and saw that the hail curtain had worn threadbare, and that the sky was lightening with the promise of the Sun.

'I looked up again at the crouching white shape, and the full temerity of my voyage came suddenly upon me. What might appear when that hazy curtain was altogether withdrawn? What might not have happened to men? What if cruelty had grown into a common passion? What if in this interval the race had lost its manliness and had developed into something inhuman, unsympathetic, and overwhelmingly powerful? I might seem some old-world savage animal, only the more dreadful and disgusting for our common likeness – a foul creature to be incontinently slain.

'Already I saw other vast shapes – huge buildings with intricate parapets and tall columns, with a wooded hill-side dimly creeping in upon me through the lessening storm. I was seized with a panic fear. I turned frantically to the Time Machine, and strove hard to readjust it. As I did so the shafts of the sun smote through the thunderstorm. The grey downpour was swept aside and vanished like the trailing garments of a ghost. Above me, in the intense blue of the summer sky, some faint brown shreds of cloud whirled into nothingness. The great buildings about me stood out clear and distinct, shining with the wet of the thunderstorm, and picked out in white by the unmelted hailstones piled along their courses. I felt naked in a strange world. I felt as perhaps a bird may feel in the clear air, knowing the hawk wings above and will swoop. My fear grew to frenzy. I took a breathing space, set my teeth, and again grappled fiercely, wrist and knee, with the machine. It gave under my desperate onset and turned over. It struck my chin violently. One hand on the saddle, the other on the lever, I stood panting heavily in attitude to mount again.

'But with this recovery of a prompt retreat my courage recovered. I looked more curiously and less fearfully at this world of the remote future. In a circular opening, high up in the wall of the nearer house, I saw a group of figures clad in rich soft robes. They had seen me, and their faces were directed towards me.

'Then I heard voices approaching me. Coming through the bushes by the White Sphinx were the heads and shoulders of men running. One of these emerged in a pathway leading straight to the little lawn upon which I stood with my machine. He was a slight creature – perhaps four feet high – clad in a purple tunic, girdled at the waist with a leather belt. Sandals or buskins – I could not clearly distinguish which – were on his feet; his legs were bare to the knees, and his head was bare. Noticing that, I noticed for the first time how warm the air was.

'He struck me as being a very beautiful and graceful creature, but indescribably frail. His flushed face reminded me of the more beautiful kind of consumptive – that hectic beauty of which we used to hear so much. At the sight of him I suddenly regained confidence. I took my hands from the machine.

Joseph Conrad's *Lord Jim*

Printed in 1900 in London. Available on Project Gutenberg at https://www.gutenberg.org/ebooks/5658/ [last access 27.11.2024].

Image 15: John Martin, "Sadak in Search of the Waters of Oblivion," 1812.

About *Lord Jim*
The Polish-born novelist Joseph Conrad (1857–1924) curiously, wrote all of his literary output in English, which was not his first nor his second language. A sailor as a young man, much of Con-

rad's work concerns men aboard and around ships, venturing out far beyond England into the territories colonized by the European powers abroad. His work is complex, and at times deliberately hard to interpret: Conrad is considered one of the earliest literary modernists, the movement that would come into its fullness as authors such as James Joyce, Virginia Woolf, and T.S. Eliot would take up the pen in the years following the turn of the twentieth century. Interpretations of Conrad range widely: sometimes considered an imperial writer, often read as critical of imperialism and colonialism broadly, Conrad's unique blend of modernism and literary impressionism presents many questions and, often, very few answers. His 1900 novel *Lord Jim* is one such frustrating text. It is a coming-of-age novel gone wrong, or perhaps a novel with a world so amoral and indifferent that coming-of-age into a respectable and noble man is an impossible enterprise. Its psychological portrayal of the two men at its center, the titular Jim and his friend and benefactor Marlow, launches from a shocking non-event, as Jim abandons his post aboard a ship that he believes will sink imminently, but which does not. From here, further ill-fated ventures play out, and Jim, far from home, must try to redeem this initial failure.

Now on to the novel . . .

Chapter IV

A month or so afterwards, when Jim, in answer to pointed questions, tried to tell honestly the truth of this experience, he said, speaking of the ship: 'She went over whatever it was as easy as a snake crawling over a stick.' The illustration was good: the questions were aiming at facts, and the official Inquiry was being held in the police court of an Eastern port. He stood elevated in the witness-box, with burning cheeks in a cool lofty room: the big framework of punkahs moved gently to and fro high above his head, and from below many eyes were looking at him out of dark faces, out of white faces, out of red faces, out of faces attentive, spellbound, as if all these people sitting in orderly rows upon narrow benches had been enslaved by the fascination of his voice. It was very loud, it rang startling in his own ears, it was the only sound audible in the world, for the terribly distinct questions that extorted his answers seemed to shape themselves in anguish and pain within his breast, – came to him poignant and silent like the terrible questioning of one's conscience. Outside the court the sun blazed – within was the wind of great punkahs that made you shiver, the shame that made you burn, the attentive eyes whose glance stabbed. The face of the presiding magistrate, clean shaved and impassible, looked at him deadly pale between the red faces of the two nautical assessors. The light of a broad window under the ceiling fell from above on the heads and shoulders of the three men, and they were fiercely distinct in the half-light of the big court-room where the audience seemed composed of staring shadows. They wanted facts. Facts! They demanded facts from him, as if facts could explain anything!

'After you had concluded you had collided with something floating awash, say a water-logged wreck, you were ordered by your captain to go forward and ascertain if there was any damage done. Did you think it likely from the force of the blow?' asked the assessor sitting to the left. He had a thin horseshoe beard, salient cheek-bones, and with both elbows on the desk clasped his rugged hands before his face, looking at Jim with thoughtful blue eyes; the other, a heavy, scornful man, thrown back in his seat, his left arm extended full length, drummed delicately with his finger-tips on a blotting-pad: in the middle the magistrate upright in the roomy arm-chair, his head inclined slightly on the shoulder, had his arms crossed on his breast and a few flowers in a glass vase by the side of his inkstand.

'I did not,' said Jim. 'I was told to call no one and to make no noise for fear of creating a panic. I thought the precaution reasonable. I took one of the lamps that were hung under the awnings and went forward. After opening the forepeak hatch I heard splashing in there. I lowered then the lamp the whole drift of its lanyard, and saw that the forepeak was more than half full of water already. I knew then there must be a big hole below the water-line.' He paused.

'Yes,' said the big assessor, with a dreamy smile at the blotting-pad; his fingers played incessantly, touching the paper without noise.

'I did not think of danger just then. I might have been a little startled: all this happened in such a quiet way and so very suddenly. I knew there was no other bulkhead in the ship but the collision bulkhead separating the forepeak from the forehold. I went back to tell the captain. I came upon the second engineer getting up at the foot of the bridge-ladder: he seemed dazed, and told me he thought his left arm was broken; he had slipped on the top step when getting down while I was forward. He exclaimed, "My God! That rotten bulkhead'll give way in a minute, and the damned thing will go down under us like a lump of lead." He pushed me away with his right arm and ran before me up the ladder, shouting as he climbed. His left arm hung by his side. I followed up in time to see the captain rush at him and knock him down flat on his back. He did not strike him again: he stood bending over him and speaking angrily but quite low. I fancy he was asking him why the devil he didn't go and stop the engines, instead of making a row about it on deck. I heard him say, "Get up! Run! fly!" He swore also. The engineer slid down the starboard ladder and bolted round the skylight to the engine-room companion which was on the port side. He moaned as he ran . . . .'

He spoke slowly; he remembered swiftly and with extreme vividness; he could have reproduced like an echo the moaning of the engineer for the better information of these men who wanted facts. After his first feeling of revolt he had come round to the view that only a meticulous precision of statement would bring out the true horror behind the appalling face of things. The facts those men were so eager to know had been visible, tangible, open to the senses, occupying their place in space and time, requiring for their existence a fourteen-hundred-ton steamer and twenty-seven minutes by the watch; they made a whole that had features, shades of expression, a complicated aspect that could be remembered by the eye, and something else besides, something invisible, a directing spirit of perdition that dwelt within, like a malevolent soul in a detestable body. He was anxious to make this clear. This had not been a common affair, everything in it had been of the utmost importance, and fortunately he remembered everything. He wanted to go on talking for truth's sake, perhaps for his own sake also; and while his utterance was deliberate, his mind positively flew round and round the serried circle of facts that had surged up all about him to cut him off from the rest of his kind: it was like a creature that, finding itself imprisoned within an enclosure of high stakes, dashes round and round, distracted in the night, trying to find a weak spot, a crevice, a place to scale, some opening through which it may squeeze itself and escape. This awful activity of mind made him hesitate at times in his speech . . . .

'The captain kept on moving here and there on the bridge; he seemed calm enough, only he stumbled several times; and once as I stood speaking to him he walked right into me as though he had been stone-blind. He made no definite answer to what I had to tell. He mumbled to himself; all I heard of it were a few words that sounded like "confounded steam!" and "infernal steam!" – something about steam. I thought . . .'

He was becoming irrelevant; a question to the point cut short his speech, like a pang of pain, and he felt extremely discouraged and weary. He was coming to that, he was coming to that – and now, checked brutally, he had to answer by yes or no. He answered truthfully by a curt 'Yes, I did'; and fair of face, big of frame, with young, gloomy eyes, he held his shoulders upright above the box while his soul writhed within him. He was made to answer another question so much to the point and so useless, then waited again. His mouth was tastelessly dry, as though he had been eating dust, then salt and bitter as after a drink of sea-water. He wiped his damp forehead, passed his tongue over parched lips, felt a shiver run down his back. The big assessor had dropped his eyelids, and drummed on without a sound, careless and mournful; the eyes of the other above the sunburnt, clasped fingers seemed to glow with kindliness; the magistrate had swayed forward; his pale face hovered near the flowers, and then dropping sideways over the arm of his chair, he rested his temple in the palm of his hand. The wind of the punkahs eddied down on the heads, on the dark-faced natives wound about in voluminous draperies, on the Europeans sitting together very hot and in drill suits that seemed to fit them as close as their skins, and holding their round pith hats on their knees; while gliding along the walls the court peons, buttoned tight in long white coats, flitted rapidly to and fro, running on bare toes, red-sashed, red turban on head, as noiseless as ghosts, and on the alert like so many retrievers.

Jim's eyes, wandering in the intervals of his answers, rested upon a white man who sat apart from the others, with his face worn and clouded, but with quiet eyes that glanced straight, interested and clear. Jim answered another question and was tempted to cry out, 'What's the good of this! what's the good!' He tapped with his foot slightly, bit his lip, and looked away over the heads. He met the eyes of the white man. The glance directed at him was not the fascinated stare of the others. It was an act of intelligent volition. Jim between two questions forgot himself so far as to find leisure for a thought. This fellow – ran the thought – looks at me as though he could see somebody or something past my shoulder. He had come across that man before – in the street perhaps. He was positive he had never spoken to him. For days, for many days, he had spoken to no one, but had held silent, incoherent, and endless converse with himself, like a prisoner alone in his cell or like a wayfarer lost in a wilderness. At present he was answering questions that did not matter though they had a purpose, but he doubted whether he would ever again speak out as long as he lived. The sound of his own truthful statements confirmed his deliberate opinion that speech was of no use to him any longer. That man there seemed to be aware of his hopeless difficulty. Jim looked at him, then turned away resolutely, as after a final parting.

And later on, many times, in distant parts of the world, Marlow showed himself willing to remember Jim, to remember him at length, in detail and audibly.

Perhaps it would be after dinner, on a verandah draped in motionless foliage and crowned with flowers, in the deep dusk speckled by fiery cigar-ends. The elongated bulk of each cane-chair harboured a silent listener. Now and then a small red glow would move abruptly, and expanding light up the fingers of a languid hand, part of a face in profound repose, or flash a crimson gleam into a pair of pensive eyes overshadowed by a fragment of an unruffled forehead; and with the very first word uttered Marlow's body, extended at rest in the seat, would become very still, as though his spirit had winged its way back into the lapse of time and were speaking through his lips from the past.

Additional Novels

These additional novels are available pull text on Project Gutenberg. HathiTrust at (hathitrust.com) hosts full facsimiles of the first editions of most of these books.

Doyle, Arthur Conan. *The Sign of the Four*. London: Spencer Blackett, 1890. Project Gutenberg. http://www.gutenberg.org/ebooks/2097 [last access 27.11.2024].
Gissing, George. *The Nether World*. 3 vols. London: Smith, Elder & Co., 1889. Project Gutenberg. https://www.gutenberg.org/ebooks/4301 [last access 27.11.2024].
Hardy, Thomas. *Jude the Obscure*. London: Osgood, McIlvaine, & Co., 1895. Project Gutenberg. http://www.gutenberg.org/ebooks/153 [last access 27.11.2024].
Hardy, Thomas. *Tess of the d'Urbervilles: Tess of the d'Ubervilles: A Pure Woman*. London: James R. Osgood, McIlvaine & Co., 1891. Project Gutenberg. http://www.gutenberg.org/ebooks/110 [last access 27.11.2024].
Levy, Amy. *The Romance of a Shop*. Boston: Cupples and Hurd, 1889. Project Gutenberg. http://www.gutenberg.org/ebooks/57447 [last access 27.11.2024].
Stevenson, Robert Louis. *The Strange Case of Dr. Jekyll and Mr. Hyde*. London: Longmans, Green and Co., 1886. Project Gutenberg. http://www.gutenberg.org/ebooks/42 [last access 27.11.2024].
Stoker, Bram. *Dracula*. New York: Grosset & Dunlap, 1897. Project Gutenberg. http://www.gutenberg.org/ebooks/345 [last access 27.11.2024].
Ward, Humphry. *Robert Elsmere*. London: Macmillan and Co., 1888. Project Gutenberg. https://www.gutenberg.org/ebooks/24898 [last access 27.11.2024].

Secondary Texts

Stickney Ellis, Sarah. "Characteristics of the Women of England." In *The Women of England*, 13–34. London, 1839; Google Books, https://books.google.com/[last access 27.11.2024].

Engels, Frederick. "The Great Towns." In *The Condition of the Working-Class in England in 1844*, Translated by Florence Kelley Wischnewetzky, 23–74. London, 1844. Project Gutenberg. https://gutenberg.org/ebooks/17306 [last access 27.11.2024].

Carlyle, Thomas. "No. VII: Hudson's Statue." In *Latter Day Pamphlets*. London, 1850; *History of Economic Thought*. https://www.hetwebsite.net/ [last access 27.11.2024].

Mayhew, Henry. *London Labour and the London Poor*. London, 1861; Internet Archive. https://archive.org/ [last access 27.11.2024].

Prince Albert. "Speech at the Banquet given at the Mansion House to the Ministers, Foreign Ambassadors, Commissioners of the Exhibition of 1851." In *The Speeches and Addresses of His Royal Highness the Prince Consort*, 109–114. London, 1862. Project Gutenberg. https://www.gutenberg.org/ebooks/61205/ [last access 27.11.2024].

Collins, Wilkie. "The Unknown Public." In *My Miscellanies*. London, 1863. Project Gutenberg. https://www.gutenberg.org/ebooks/43893/ [last access 27.11.2024].

Mill, John Stuart. *The Subjection of Women*. London, 1869. Project Gutenberg. https://www.gutenberg.org/ebooks/27083 [last access 27.11.2024].

Darwin, Charles. *On the Origin of Species*. London, 1872. Project Gutenberg. https://www.gutenberg.org/ebooks/1228 [last access 27.11.2024].

Eliot, George. "The Natural History of German Life" and "Silly Novels by Lady Novelists." In *The Essays of 'George Eliot'*, edited by Nathan Sheppard. New York, 1883. Project Gutenberg. https://www.gutenberg.org/ebooks/28289 [last access 27.11.2024].

Wilde, Oscar. "The Critic as Artist" and "The Truth of Masks." In *Intentions*. London, 1891. Project Gutenberg. https://www.gutenberg.org/ebooks/887 [last access 27.11.2024].

Wilde, Oscar. *The Soul of Man*. London: Arthur L. Humphrey, 1900. Project Gutenberg. https://www.gutenberg.org/ebooks/1017 [last access 27.11.2024].

Marx, Karl. "Commodities." In *A Contribution to the Critique of Political Economies*. Translated by N.I. Stone, 19–55. Chicago: Charles H. Kerr and Co., 1904. Project Gutenberg. https://www.gutenberg.org/ebooks/46423 [last access 27.11.2024].

Chesterton, G.K.. *Charles Dickens: A Critical Study*. United States, 1911. Project Gutenberg. https://www.gutenberg.org/ebooks/68682 [last access 27.11.2024].

Forster, E.M.. "Flat and Round Characters." In *Aspects of the Novel*, 103–118. New York, 1927. Internet Archive. https://archive.org/ [last access 27.11.2024].

Further Reading

The follow scholarship invaluable for understanding the included novels in their contexts. Due to copyright restrictions, however, these texts cannot be reproduced in this reader.

Armstrong, Nancy. *Desire and Domestic Fiction: A Political History of the Novel*. Oxford: Oxford University Press, 1987.

Auerbach, Erich. "In the Hotel de la Mole." In *Mimesis*: *The Representation of Reality in Western Literature*. Translated by Willard R. Trask, 454–492. Princeton, NJ: Princeton University Press, 2014.

Bakhtin, M.M.. *The Dialogic Imagination: Four Essays*, trans. By Caryl Emerson and Michael Holquist. Austin: University of Texas Press, 1986.

Benjamin, Walter. "The Storyteller. In *Illuminations*, Translated by Harcourt Brace Jovanovich, Inc, 83–110. New York: Schocken Books, 2008.

Friedgood, Elaine. *Worlds Enough: The Invention of Realism in the Victorian Novel*. Princeton, NJ: Princeton University Press, 2019.

Moretti, Franco. *The Way of the World: The Bildungsroman in European Culture*. New York: Verso, 2000.

Price, Leah. *How to do Things with Books in Victorian Britain*. Princeton: Princeton University Press, 2012.

Watt, Ian. *The Rise of the Novel*. Berkeley: University of California Press, 2001.

Online Resources and Databases

The Victorian Web,
https://victorianweb.org/ [last access 27.11.2024]
A helpful database which is both informative and easily navigable on many aspects of Victorian culture, literature, technology, and history.

Measuring Worth,
https://eh.net/howmuchisthat/ [last access 27.11.2024]
A series of converters for sums of money to and from various currencies and through the last several hundred years.

At the Circulating Library,
https://www.victorianresearch.org/atcl/index.php [last access 27.11.2024]
A very comprehensive bibliography of Victorian fiction which boasts over twenty-two thousand entries.

Reading Like a Victorian,
https://readinglikeavictorian.osu.edu/ [last access 27.11.2024]
A timeline which shows which texts were being serially published concurrently during the Victorian period.

Dickens Search,
https://dickenssearch.com/ [last access 27.11.2024]
A fusion of book history and digital tools which provides the fully searchable Dickens canon.

Darwin Online,
http://darwin-online.org.uk/majorworks.html [last access 27.11.2024]
The virtual home of all of Charles Darwin's major writings.

Victorian Women Writers,
https://webapp1.dlib.indiana.edu/vwwp [last access 27.11.2024]
An ongoing project creating a database of Victorian women writers, including lesser-known writers and writers who receive little scholarly attention.

Charles Booth's 1889 Map of London Poverty,
http://websites.umich.edu/~risotto/ [last access 27.11.2024]
A descriptive map of London's poverty and the London poor.

Appendix I: Timeline of England's Wars

Adapted from Byron Farwell's *Queen Victoria's Little Wars*.

1802	End of the French Revolutionary Wars
1802–1805	Second Anglo-Maratha War
1802–1813	Napoleonic Wars y
1812–1815	War of 1812
1815	Hundred Days
1813–1816	Anglo-Nepalese War
1817–1818	Third Anglo-Maratha War
1823–1831	First Ashanti War
1824–1826	First Anglo-Burmese War
1839–1842	First Anglo-Afghan War
1839–1842	First Opium War
1840	First Anglo Marri War
1845–1846	First Anglo-Sikh War
1845–1872	New Zealand Wars
1848–1849	Second Anglo-Sikh War
1852–1853	Second Anglo-Burmese War
1853–1856	Crimean War
1856–1857	Anglo-Persian War
1856–1860	Second Opium War
1857–1858	Indian Rebellion
1863–1864	Second Ashanti War
1864–1865	Bhutan War
1873–1874	Third Ashanti War
1878–1880	Second Anglo-Afghan War
1879	Anglo-Zulu War
1880	Second Anglo Marri War
1880–1881	First Boer War
1885	Third Anglo-Burmese War
1881–1899	Mahdist War
1894	Fourth Ashanti War
1896	Anglo-Zanzibar War
1899	Six-Day War
1899–1901	Boxer Rebellion
1899–1902	Second Boer War

Appendix II: England's Domestic Timeline

1801	Act of Union with Ireland
1810–1820	Regency of the Prince of Wales
1817	Death of Princess Charlotte of Wales
1820	Ascension of George IV
1820–1830	Reign of George IV
1824	Repeal of the Combination Acts
1825	Railway opens between Stockton and Darlington: first passenger rail in history
1828	Repeal of the Test and Corporation Acts
1829	Catholic Emancipation Act
1832	First Reform Act Passed
1833	Act for the Emancipation of all Slaves
1833	Factory Act passed to protect child workers
1834	Poor Law Act
1837	Ascension of Queen Victoria
1839–1901	Reign of Queen Victoria
1839	Establishment of penny postage
1840	Canadian Act of Union
1842	Free Trade Budget
1848	Chartist Rising
1848	Irish Rebellion
1850	Tennyson made poet laureate
1859	Darwin published *Origin of Species*
1865	Election of liberal majority in parliament
1867	Second Reform Act
1872	Ballot Act
1874	Election of conservative majority in parliament
1875	Public Health Act, Artisans' Dwelling Act, Trade Union Act
1876	Victoria becomes Empress of India
1876	Invention of Telephone
1880–1885	Gladstone Ministry (second)
1884	Third Reform Act
1887	Golden Jubilee of Queen Victoria
1891	Elementary education made free and compulsory
1895	Election of unionist majority in parliament
1897	Diamond Jubilee of Queen Victoria
1897	Women's Compensation Act
1901	Death of Queen Victoria

Editor's Statement

As of 2024, Dan Dougherty was a Postdoctoral Fellow at the University of Florida Writing Program who recently received his PhD from Boston College in English Literature. Dougherty writes on the intersection of radical form and the anglophone novel, and also develops pedagogical resources including lesson plans, topic readers, and guides on burgeoning technologies. His ongoing project reorients the coming-of-age novel in new constellations that cross-national borders and conventionally defined literary periods stemming from a shared commitment to generic fusions of other literary genres that inflect and distort the teleological development plots. His work has appeared in *Brontë Studies*, *College Teaching*, *The Journal of the Scholarship of Teaching and Learning*, and *The Journal of Modern Literature*, amongst other venues.

Index

Acquaintance 10, 34, 63, 76
Animal(s)
– Bat(s) 52
– Bird(s) 43, 71
– Canary 34
– Cygnet 62
– Dog(s) 12–14, 26, 35, 46, 72
– Dormouse 50–55
– Duck(s) 62
– Elephant 41
– Hare 50–54
– Horse(s) 31, 67
– Mouse 34
– Pea-chicks 26
– Raven 50
– Rook(s) 42–43
– Sheep 26
– Snake(s) 88
– Sparrow(s) 79
Art 15, 69–71, 73, 75, 77–80
– Dancing 30, 32, 37, 84
– Drawing 14, 32, 35–36, 54, 64, 77, 79
– Painting 77–78, 83
– Portrait 71–72, 74, 78
– Statue 84
Austen, Jane 5–6
– *Pride and Prejudice* 6, 10

Beauty 8, 16, 25, 34, 42, 55, 66, 70–72, 75, 77–80, 86
– Handsome 8, 26, 40, 62
– Lovliness 78
British Empire 5, 21, 59
Brontë, Charlotte 23
– Jane Eyre (character) 21
– *Jane Eyre* 2, 22
Byron, George Gordon 12

Carroll, Lewis 49
– *Alice's Adventures in Wonderland* 49
Charm 34, 63, 70, 78–79
Children 8, 21, 24, 26–28, 30, 32–33, 36, 40, 42, 44–45, 49, 61, 74
– Bab(ies) 39, 48

– Boy(s) 44, 48, 72, 76
– Girl(s) 7–8, 10, 23–24, 26, 30, 32, 34, 36, 43–44, 61, 63, 67
– Orphan 35, 39, 45
Children's Literature 21, 49
Chimne(ies) 13, 24–25
Christian 33, 41, 63
– Church(es) 27, 44, 72
– Clergy 63–64, 72
Class 21
– Aristocracy 2
– Lower 2
– Middle 2
– Nobility 31
– Royalty 5, 52
– Social standing 7
– Upper 2, 5, 7, 23, 34, 71, 75, 79, 82, 85
Collins, Wilkie 21
Colour 24, 74, 78–79, 83
– Black 31–32, 72, 83
– Blue 72, 74, 79, 83, 85, 89
– Brown 62, 74, 77, 83, 85
– Crimson 24, 91
– Green 79, 83–84
– Red 24–26, 28, 32, 34, 47, 75, 88, 91
– White 24–25, 27, 40–41, 62, 73–74, 76, 83–85, 88, 91
Conrad, Joseph 87
– *Lord Jim* 87
Conversation 15, 51, 79
Creature(s) 13, 15, 34, 36, 66–67, 72, 80, 85–86, 90
Cruel 40, 59, 85

Danger 16, 89
Dark 1, 13, 15, 25–27, 40, 47, 82, 88, 90
Darwin, Charles 97
– *On the Origin of Species* 101
Death 15, 24–25, 27, 32, 34, 40–41, 43, 45, 59, 67–68
– Coffin 25
– Funeral 42
Decadent Movement 59
Depression 26, 64

https://doi.org/10.1515/9783111561547-024

Index

Destiny. *See* Fate 17
Dickens, Charles 2, 21, 30, 38, 97
– Pip (character) 21
– *David Copperfield* 2, 38
Drawing-room 32, 35–36, 64, 67
Drug(s)
– Cigar 91
– Cigarettes 71, 79
– Laudanum 47
– Opium 1, 72

Early Victorian
– Nation 21
– War 21
Eat(ing) 26, 30, 53, 62, 90
Education 15, 37, 45, 70
– Academy for young ladies 31
– Drawing 54
– Literacy 65–66
– School(s) 33, 35, 47, 77
– Student(s) 32–35
Ego-document(s)
– Autobiography 70, 78
– Journal 14
– Letter(s) 15, 32–33, 35, 65–66
– Narrative(s) 17
Eighteenth century 5, 7
Eliot, George 60
– *Middlemarch* 60
Eliot, T.S. 88
Eloquence 15
Emotion 7, 15, 17, 26, 30, 39, 65, 67, 70, 74–75, 79, 83–84
– Admiration 15
– Anger 50–51, 54, 79, 89
– Benevolence 31
– Cowardice 75
– Curiosity 14–15, 17, 50–51, 83
– Delight 8, 26, 63, 78
– Desire 8, 16–17, 33, 65
– Despair 14–16, 61
– Desperation 23
– Eagerness 14, 17
– Enthusiasm 16
– Fear 17, 25, 34–35, 44–45, 64, 85, 89
– Gloomy 14–15, 25, 27, 90
– Grief 15–16, 67
– Happiness 15–16, 32, 44, 47–48, 62–64, 67, 77
– Horror 27, 89
– Humour 34
– Indifferent 73, 76, 79
– Joy(s) 75
– Madness 13, 15, 78, 83
– Melancholy 14, 17, 30–31, 48, 63
– Misery 15–16, 33
– Mournful 90
– Nervous 9, 33, 42, 75
– Pity 15
– Regret 67
– Sentimental 31, 35
– Sorrow 27, 62, 67, 75
– Sympathy 14–17, 63, 70, 76, 85
– Uneasy 14, 44, 63
– Unhappy 15
– Weep(ing) 36
– Wildness 13
England 1, 5, 7, 21, 30–31, 40, 72
– London 70
– Oxford 72
English 21, 32, 51, 76–77
Entertainment 21
– Club 35
– Pub 21
Epistolary 12, 32
Europe 5, 13, 88
– Europeans 90
– France 5
– Lake Geneva 12
– Poland 87
– Spain 5
European continent *See* Europe 5

Faith 39, 61, 63
Family 27, 30–31, 33–34, 39–41, 45, 62
– Aunt(s) 28, 40–41, 43, 45–48, 79–80
– Brother(s) 14–15, 27, 61, 76
– Daughter(s) 7–9, 32, 34, 45
– Father(s) 9–10, 40–42, 67
– Grandpapa 35
– Mother(s) 9, 23, 25–27, 40–48, 67, 76
– Sister(s) 8, 25, 27, 32–34, 36, 53–54, 67
Farwell, Byron
– *Queen Victoria's Little Wars* 99
Fashion 33, 36

- Bonnet 35, 46, 48
- Cane 77, 91
- Coat(s) 74, 78, 91
- Coiffure 61
- Cork jackets 39
- Dress 26, 42, 44
- Hat(s) 9, 31, 76, 91
- Jewellery 46
- Robe(s) 85
- Silver case 79
- Tunic(s) 86
- Waistcoat(s) 32
Fate 17, 39, 64, 67, 75
Fatigue 10, 13, 65
Fin de siècle 59
Fire 25, 40–47, 65, 83
Food
- Butter 51, 53
- Dinner 10, 30, 52, 91
- Gingerbread 30
- Luncheon 79
- Sandwich(es) 36
- Sea Water 90
- Soup 13
- Treacle 53–54
- Water 32, 40, 54, 89
- Wine 35, 50
French 5, 23, 36
Friend(s) 16, 76
Friendship 9, 15–17, 32, 35, 44, 68, 72, 75–76, 79–80

Garden(s) 36, 41, 43, 55, 71, 73, 78–80, 82, 84
Gaskell, Elizabeth 2
Genre
- Coming-of-age 23, 39, 59, 88
- Detective Stories 1–2
- Epistolary 12
- Fairy Tales 21
- Ghost(s) stories 1
- Gothic literature 12
- Gothic novel 23, 69
- Historical novel(s) 1, 5
- Horror 1
- Impressionism 88
- Marriage plot 1
- Poetry 62

- Satire 81
- Speculative fiction 1, 5, 81
- Thriller 69
Godwin, William 12
Grief 14–17, 27, 34–35

Health 14, 34
Heart 15–16, 24, 26–27, 33–34, 36, 42, 61–62, 68, 74, 78–79
Heroine(s) 5, 21, 34, 60
History 16–17, 34, 39, 61, 73, 77, 97
Home 24, 31, 35, 41
Homosexuality 70
Human 12–13, 44, 61
- Nobility 16
Humour 9, 30–31
- Riddle 51

Illness 9, 15, 28, 34, 41, 45–46, 53, 61, 65, 67
- Cough 9
- Emaciation 13
- Indisposition 45
- Scarlet Fever 32
Imperialism 88
India 41
Inequalit(ies) 12, 21
Ireland 5

Johnson, Samuel 33
- Dictionary 33
Joyce, James 88

Kitchen(s) 13, 25

Late Victorian 57
Latin 64, 66
Librar(ies) 1, 21, 64, 66–67
Life 2, 9–10, 13–16, 21, 31, 33–35, 39–40, 42, 44, 55, 61, 63, 70, 73, 75, 77–80
Light 13, 27–28, 31, 40, 46–48, 61, 71, 79, 83–85, 88, 91
- Candle(s) 31, 40, 44, 46
Literacy 1
- Reading 1, 10, 17, 21, 63–66, 70
London 1–2, 11, 21, 33, 59, 71, 97
Love 8, 14, 26–27, 31, 34, 62, 68, 73, 79
- Affection(s) 44

– Ardor 61, 64
– Ardour 15
– Familial 10
– Language of the heart 15
– Making 30

Manuscript 17
Marriage 5, 7–9, 23, 32, 40–41, 45, 62, 64, 66–67, 73
– Divorce 76
– Husband 25, 27, 33, 40, 63, 65–67, 73
– Wife 7–10, 30, 33, 62–63, 73
Men 1, 7–10, 12–16, 25, 27, 30, 33, 35, 46–47, 62–63, 67, 70–73, 75–80, 84–85, 88–89, 91
Mirror(s) 25, 27, 70
Modern 1, 73, 79
Modernism 88
Money 13, 24, 33, 39, 45, 73, 97
– Crown 40
– Pence 33, 40
– Pound(s) 32, 39, 45
– Shilling(s) 21, 32, 40
– Sovereign 32
Music 32, 52
– Piano 76
– Singing 16, 24, 34, 52
– Violin(s) 76

Narrative(s) 2, 17, 21
Nation 1, 5, 21
Naturalism 59
Nature 17, 27, 61, 80
– Air 13, 59, 74, 83–86
– Day 9–10, 14–15, 17, 25, 34–35, 39, 47, 51, 66, 77–79, 82–83
– Hail 84–85
– Ice 12–14
– Moon 27, 54, 83
– Moors 25
– Night 1, 13, 17, 26, 39–40, 45, 82–83, 90
– Ocean 15
– Rain 84–85
– Sea(s) 12–13, 16, 39, 41, 43
– Sk(ies) 16, 52, 76, 83, 85
– Snow 83

– Sun 41, 83, 85, 88
– Weather 12, 35, 85
Newspaper(s) 39, 75
Nineteenth century 1–2, 5, 7, 21, 59, 70, 75
North Pole 13
Novel 1, 21, 35, 59
Nurser(ies) 25–26, 28, 45

Pamphlet(s) 63
Parliament 5
– Debate(s) 2
– Rotten boroughs' 5
Parlour 34, 36, 40, 42, 44, 46–47
Peace 17, 43
Peril 14
Phantom(s)
– Fairy 25, 48
– Ghost(s) 1, 12, 28, 39, 85, 91
– Spirit 16
– Spirit(s) 27
– Supernatural 48, 70
Philosopher(s) 5
Pity 27–28, 63, 79
Plant(s)
– Conservatory 26
– Dais(ies) 74–76
– Elm-trees 43
– Flower(s) 35, 55, 62, 72, 78, 89–91
– Geranium 32
– Grass(es) 71, 73–74, 79
– Laburnum 71
– Lilac(s) 71, 74
– Mushroom 55
– Rhododendron 84
– Silver birch 85
– Tree(s) 55, 71, 74, 83
– Vines 26
– Woodbine 71
Polidori, John 12
Politic(s)
– Democracy 76
Poor. *See* Poverty 21
Poorhouse 24
Poverty 70, 97
– Lodging house(s) 79
Power 16–17, 26, 59, 76

Press 31
Pre-Victorian
– Acts of Union 5
– Battle of Trafalgar 5
– French Revolution 5
– Industrial Revolution 5
– Napoleonic Wars 5
– Philosophical Revolution 5
– Reform Act
　– First 5
Prose 7, 62, 70
Protagonist(s) 2
Public IV, 1, 31, 63, 71, 74
Punch (periodical) 30
Punish(ment) 23–24, 27
Puppet Master 21

Queen Victoria 5, 21
– Death 59

Realism 7
Religion 33, 47, 61–64
– Mythology 63
Romance 73, 79

Saint Theresa 61–62
Salon(s) 76
Science 12, 61, 82
– Chemistry 84
– Discovery 13
– Geography 32
– Laborator(ies) 82–83
– Quacks 30
Science Fiction *See* Speculative Fiction
Scotland 40
Scott, Walter
– *Waverley* 5
Shelley, Mary 12
– *Frankenstein* 5, 11
Shelley, Percy Bysshe 12
Sherlock Holmes 2
Sixteenth century 62
Skin 26, 35, 84
Slavery
– Abolished 5
Social commentary 2
Society 5, 21, 30, 46, 61–62, 74, 82

– Civilization 84
Soul 15–17, 26, 61, 63, 66, 74–75, 77–79, 90
Speculative Fiction 12
– Time Machine 82
– Time travel 83
Squalor 2
St. Kitt 34
Stoker, Bram
– *Dracula* 59
Superstition 25

Tea 40, 43–44, 50–53, 55
– Teaboard 46
Technology
– Clock(s) 1, 12, 26, 39, 42, 47, 52, 82
– Clocktowers 21
– Machine(s) 83–86
– Railroads 1, 21
– Rocket 82
– Telephone 21
– Telescope(s) 12
– Watch 51, 74, 85, 90
Temper 25, 32, 40, 65–66
Terror 37, 67, 75
Thackeray, William Makepeace 30
– *Vanity Fair* 21, 29
Traveller(s) 12–14, 25, 48
Truth 7, 17, 72, 88, 90–91
Twentieth century 59

Ugly 70, 73

Vehicle(s) 14
– Carriage 12, 35–37
– Coach 31–32, 36
– Sledge 12–15
– Waggon 30
Vessel(s)
– Ship 12–13, 88–89
– Steamer 90
Vice and Virtue 70
– Vice 76
– Virtue 32, 34, 73, 79
Victorian 1, 59
– Indian Rebellion 99
– Second Second Opium War 99
Victorian 97

Villain(s) 34
Violence 15, 25–28, 43, 70
Voyage(s) 13, 85

Wells, H.G. 81
- The Time Machine 59, 86
Wilde, Oscar 69
- *The Picture of Dorian Gray* 69
Wollstonecraft, Mary 12
Women 1, 7–10, 23, 30, 32–37, 39–42, 46–47, 61–63, 65, 68, 75, 80, 97
- Gentlewoman 32
- Spanish 61
- Womanhood 61
Woolf, Virginia 59–60, 88
Work 33, 43, 55, 64, 66, 71, 77–79
- Actor 70
- Artist(s) 31, 70–72, 74, 78, 80
- Assessor 90
- Author(s) 1, 5, 21
- Butler 66, 80
- Captain 13, 16, 89–90
- Coachman 31–32, 35–36
- Dacing master 36
- Doctor(s) 46, 66–67
- Engineer 89
- Factor(ies) 21
- Governess 45
- Hatter 50–54
- Lexicographer 33
- Magistrate 88–90
- Maid 23, 25
- Medical man 67
- Merchant 33
- Nautical assessors 88
- Nurse(s) 39, 46
- Officer 14
- Painter 70
- Painter(s) 71–72, 74, 77–78, 80
- Pick-pocket 30
- Playwright 70
- Police 30
- Politician(s) 21
- Sailor(s) 13–14, 87
- Schoolmistress 33, 35
- Scientist 82
- Servant 7, 23, 25–26, 31–32, 34, 36, 41, 80
- Stone cutter 33
- Worker(s) 2
- Writers 97

www.ingramcontent.com/pod-product-compliance
Lightning Source LLC
Jackson TN
JSHW061115250625
86703JS00004B/56

The 19th-Century British novel continues to delight readers and populate syllabi of survey courses as well as specialized electives. Because there is such a tremendous volume of literature that emerged from England during this century, this volume offers a guided, chronological tour through the century, featuring authors including Charles Dickens, George Eliot, Joseph Conrad, and many more. This volume is meant to provide a reading list for students and educators interested in these texts, including excerpts, images (some of which are taken from the novels themselves), external online resources, and appendices. In addition, this volume features links to essays by 19th-century authors contemplating their own work and position in their moment, as well as suggested reading lists for contemporary scholarship on the novel broadly construed. As an educational resource, this volume contains many of the tools and texts that are important for new readers of the 19th-century British novel as well as educators building survey courses or specialized electives with an eye towards accessibility and convenience.

THE SERIES: TINY TOPIC READER HUMANITIES
The *Tiny Topic Reader* series is an exciting new (textbook) series focused on providing focused collections of materials on a diverse range of topics. Each reader in the Tiny Topic series provides a small, curated collection of material on a specific topic. Ranging from 50 to 150 pages, these volumes are designed to offer selections for a week or more of excellent readings on diverse subjects, making them ideal for broad college survey courses or to start digging into specific topics. They include an introduction providing context for the students and researchers as well as end matter such as time lines or lists of relevant archives and other useful information for digging into the topic.

www.degruyterbrill.com
ISBN 978-3-11-156056-4
ISSN 2944-1552

DE GRUYTER

PARADIGM SHIFT

SEVENTH ANNUAL CONFERENCE 2024

Edited by Herman J. Selderhuis

EUARE LECTURES